# Yves Saint Laurent Museum Marrakech

STUDIO KO

# Yves Saint Laurent Museum Marrakech

Texts by **Catherine Sabbah**

This is a special book – even, dare I say it, a very special one – about adventure, eloquence and compassion. It is an ode to a passion for the radiant power of artistic expression and to a love for the transmission of creative traditions, and it is also a warm tribute to Morocco.

This elegant book – designed by Karl Fournier, Olivier Marty and their collaborator Fayçal Tiaïba from the Studio KO architecture agency – traces the incredible artistic process that enabled a rough, candid sketch to metamorphose like a chrysalis into a bountiful and beautiful building.

This book is particularly poignant for me. It reveals a clear portrait of the late Pierre Bergé, who, towards the end of his life, with his characteristic boundless energy, undertook a formidable task: to create an institution that would leave a lasting impression of the man he loved and serve as a legacy for the country he loved so much, one that had become his second home. In these pages, Karl Fournier and Olivier Marty have been able to capture and accurately convey Pierre Bergé's vision and spirit. We often talk about collaboration and 'synergy', but this project truly is the quintessence of these two concepts. As part of this magnificent enterprise, I had the honour of working with an impressive team that included Björn Dahlström, who was then the director of the Berber Museum; the exhibition curator Christophe Martin; and a long list of consultants, collaborators and specialists in lighting, air conditioning, humidity regulation, conservation and security. Each of us, supported by the constant efforts of Moroccan contractors and labourers, worked tirelessly to build this landmark in record time.

Unfortunately, Pierre Bergé died a few weeks before the Yves Saint Laurent Museum Marrakech opened, but his enthusiastic commitment and his pride in this project gave him a tenfold feeling of peace during his final hours. The building houses so many things he loved deeply, from the Senufo bird sculpture that greets visitors in the lobby to the impressive collection of Arab–Andalusian books in the museum's research library – not to mention the auditorium that bears his name and hosts classical music recitals, including by Moroccan musicians. This dynamic and vibrant institution is a reflection not only of Pierre Bergé's many artistic passions but also of those he cherished. It is with sincere gratitude that I thank Karl Fournier and Olivier Marty for this very special ode to love.

Madison Cox,
Marrakech 2021

To Pierre Bergé

# 1,423 days to go

It was not so surprising to receive a call from Pierre Bergé. But neither was it a common occurrence. We knew each other. But we also knew of his lack of enthusiasm for contemporary architecture. Once – only once – had we seen him stop at the site of one of the houses we were building in Morocco, Villa K, as though moved by it. He later told us that it was in that moment the light went on for him – when he understood that a carefully considered assembly of materials and forms could create art in a space and, above all, in the landscape.

That day on the phone, he invited us to dinner, without telling us more. Karl Fournier went on his own. And it was not until the dessert that he understood why he was there: Pierre Bergé wanted to build a museum dedicated to Yves Saint Laurent in Marrakech. Was this statement a request or a requirement? It is not easy to say no to Pierre Bergé, and we never even considered doing so.

He had chosen us to build, next to the unforgettable Jardin Majorelle, a place that would be a tribute to a genius of haute couture and where the memory of his companion would continue to live on. What was he wanting? 'A contemporary Moroccan building', rooted in the land that he and Yves Saint Laurent had discovered together in 1966 and then made their home. The remit was summed up in these words. It was up to us to offer him a place worthy of this talent and this love.

'Neither mausoleum nor architectural gesticulation.' That was more or less all that he said that evening. But he had instilled in us an excitement, mixed with curiosity and a sense of responsibility, that kept us on high alert for several days.

# 1,398 days to go

## Visiting the foundation

The brief was indeed brief. The contents of the museum already existed, in abundance, as Karl Fournier and Olivier Marty discovered when they visited the Pierre Bergé–Yves Saint Laurent Foundation in Paris and viewed the extremely rich collections in its storerooms. Models, objects, drawings, reference books, photos of the famous fashion designer: there was a profusion of things, memories, impressions and atmospheres to be exhibited that would reveal a world usually reserved for a happy few – and allow visitors to experience the same sense of discovery that the architects felt.

ARMOIRE N° 18
COLLECTION
AUTOMNE-HIVER
1982-83
MODÈLE N° 39
ENSEMBLE HABILLÉ
DOSSIER - 13

Architect Jean-Michel Rousseau, who had transformed the fashion house into a foundation in 2002, was in charge of the project brief and envisioned all the spaces necessary for a museum worthy of the name. The 4,000 m² (43,060 ft²) museum needed to house a permanent exhibition hall, a temporary exhibitions hall, a bookshop, a research library, an auditorium, a few offices and a cafe, not forgetting, in the basement, storage and conservation areas – the real nerve centre that would allow the place to function and succeed. It was up to the architects to imagine a layout that would ensure the most fluid and pleasant route and enhance and protect the collections.

# 1,380 days to go

## Concept design

In the architectural duo of Karl Fournier and
Olivier Marty, one creates with words, the
other designs – and, from this alchemy, projects emerge. The night following the famous
dinner was productive. Would this museum be
a literal association between architecture and
couture or the vision of a flexible and malleable
material? Karl Fournier dreamed of a brick
wall supple like fabric. Olivier Marty started
from the paradoxical idea of a lightness that
would fall perfectly like a well-cut garment.
He imagined a building placed so delicately
on the ground that its extremities would meet
it not abruptly but gently, in a curve. Both
the dream and the technique can be seen in
their preparatory drawings. In any event, the
founding principles had already germinated.
All that remained was to convert these drawings into a volume and, with the help of project
manager Fayçal Tiaïba, fit the planned project
– exhibition rooms, bookshop, auditorium,
storerooms – into it.

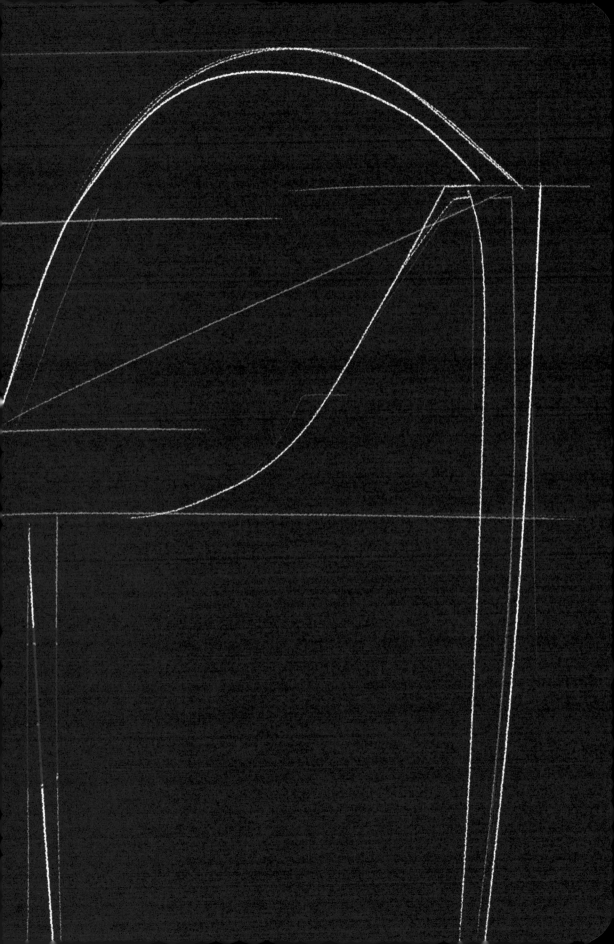

'I never knew Pierre Bergé, and this distance undoubtedly gave me more freedom of expression', Fayçal Tiaïba recalls. 'I didn't know what he would like or not like. I fumbled around a bit before launching into a rather abrupt sketch, more unyielding than what Olivier had already drawn. My line evoked the slopes of the Atlas Mountains, the ridge that would have risen when the tectonic plates met.'

The design for the museum's cantilevered auditorium was based on this alternative sketch. Following the rake of the seating and floating above the ground, it saves space on the small 2,500 m² (26,910 ft²) plot that had to accommodate the whole museum complex.

What emerged was a compact and completely opaque building – like the interior of an Arab house, which is carefully hidden from street view. It would be entered through a circular courtyard, open in the middle. The main material would be brick, worked decoratively in mashrabiya on the facade; there are 1,000 ways to use it and Moroccan artisans know them all.

'These design moments were very moving', says Madison Cox, president of the Pierre Bergé–Yves Saint Laurent Foundation. 'It was something new for everyone; Pierre Bergé had renovated houses but never built a building that had to be imagined from A to Z, and Karl and Olivier had designed splendid buildings but never a museum, which is something entirely different. We all had a lot to learn.'

'Because of the programme (exhibition galleries that needed to be windowless, the auditorium, the conservation space, etc.), I was obviously thinking of a very opaque building. A clever assembly of cubes that would reveal, in their centre, a courtyard, a place open to the sky, a garden? But, above all, and allegorically, I imagined these cubes dressed in lace-like brickwork.

This pattern would obviously be reminiscent of the weft of a fabric. Whereas, like a garment lining, the interior would be radically different – smooth and bright – the exterior would be textured, porous and coloured. Pierre wanted a strong architectural gesture; Madison insisted on the contemporary aspect. As we were leaving, Pierre walked me back to the car and said: "So, why do I want you to do it? It's simple: I want something strong; Moroccan; contemporary; and, above all, meticulously designed."

I also know – and it's something I'm enthusiastic about, too – that you've been dying to design an all-brick building for ages. OK, we're agreed, this is only the beginning of the reflection, but there's enough of a thread here for us to pick up and start knitting with, right?'

– Email from Karl Fournier to Olivier Marty,
1 November 2013, Marrakech

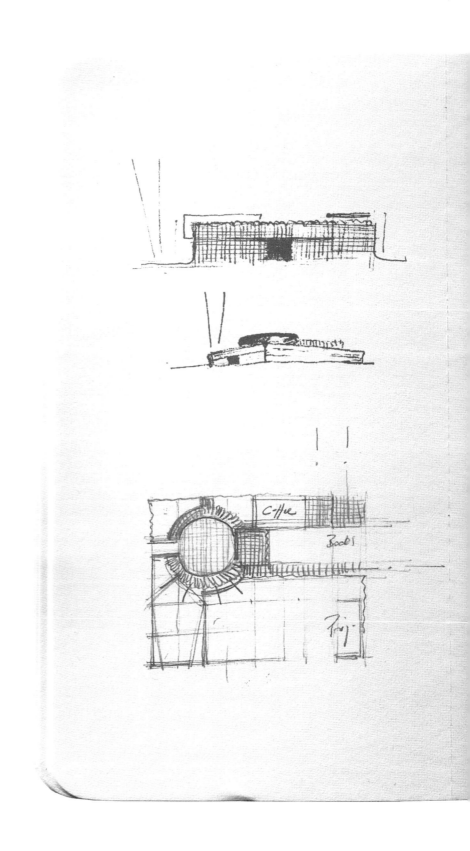

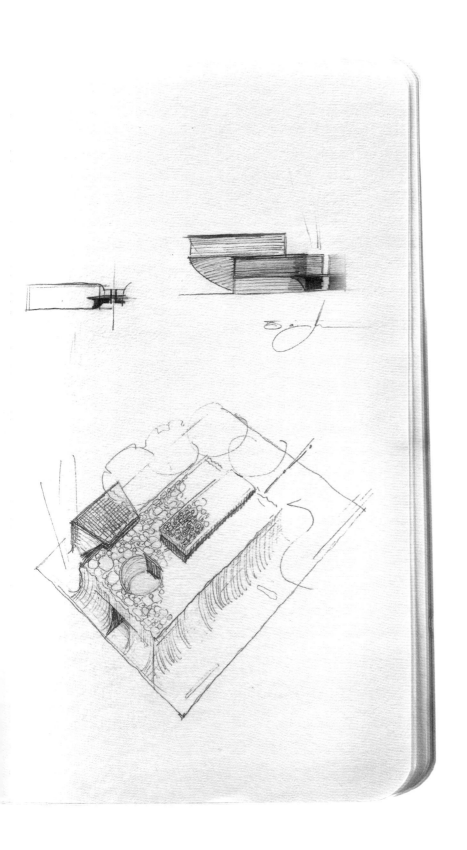

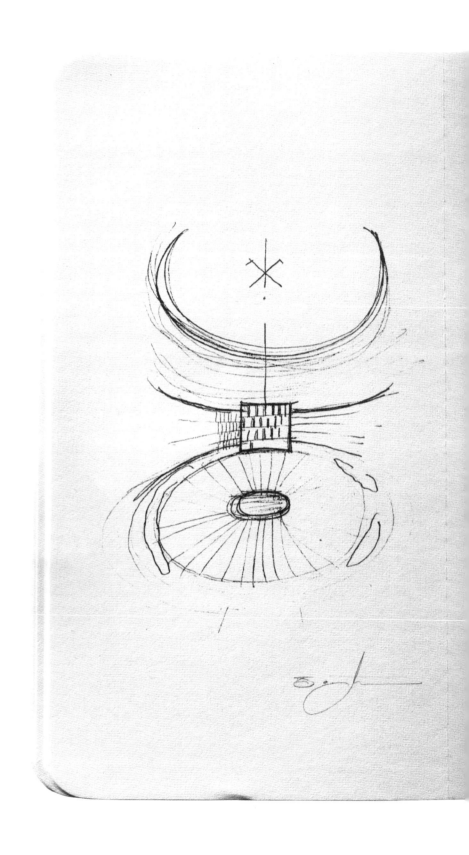

# 1,314 days to go

## The pitch

As unique as the commission was, there were
still rules to be followed. Before starting the
project, approval needed to be obtained from
the client, Pierre Bergé, and the foundation's
board. The presentation of the plan was sched-
uled for March 2014 at the headquarters in
Paris. It was a baptism of fire, confronting the
architects' vision with that of a jury that may
already have had images in their minds of a
completely different project and that were
accustomed to excellence. The building that
Studio KO had designed – simple yet radi-
cal – was equally likely to arouse unanimous
support or a brutal rejection. It was important,
therefore, to choose the right words to explain
the choice of forms and materials, without
going into too much technical detail about the
constraints that had nevertheless determined
some of the final decisions.

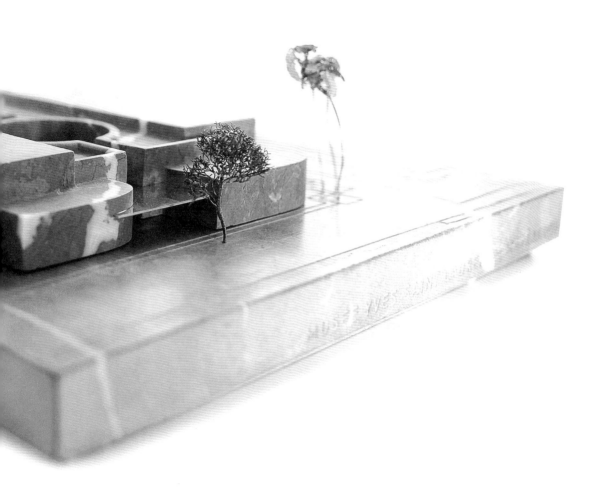

Another difficulty was that only an expert eye can grasp at first glance the subtlety of an architectural plan and how it works. The team had planned to present three perspective images drawn by the Japanese illustrator Mizuho Kishi, and they brought samples of all the materials envisaged: the brick, the colour and material of which formed the DNA of the project, as well as the woods and the terrazzo (a material made of fragments of marble agglomerated with cement, then polished to give it the sheen of natural stone) planned for a plinth under the facades. But pictures can never tell the whole story of a project. The architects had saved the best for last: a key element that serves most of their projects.

'We unveiled the model only after having explained everything, just before the end of the meeting', recalls Karl Fournier. More than just a model, the miniature museum carved from a single block of red marble is a work of art created by Italian artist Miza Mucciarelli. Visible from all angles, it conveyed much more about the volumes, proportions and colour of the place than any image could do. Pierre Bergé was won over. The members of the board were equally enthusiastic and proposed no changes. The architects realized over time, however, that behind this goodwill was a need for excellence. What everyone had seen in this meeting would remain etched on their memories until the project was completed. It was this building, in all its details, that they were required to build.

'The building we had in mind
was grounded: humble yet proud.'

– Karl Fournier

# 1,287 days to go

## A weekend in Normandy

Pierre Bergé had invited us for the weekend to his sublime dacha near Deauville, in north-western France. The atmosphere was friendly and easy-going; Quito Fierro, a very loyal friend, had made the trip from Marrakech to join us. As he liked to do sometimes, Pierre had given his staff time off and had cooked for us himself – a memorable saffron risotto. Was he looking to create an impression or did he suddenly just feel inspired? Whatever the reason, after lunch, he decided to organize a trip to Le Havre to visit the Église Saint-Joseph, a church by Auguste Perret. So, off we went in his vintage Bentley.

For those who have never visited it, which we had not, this 1950s building comes as a shock. The concrete beams that provide structure and divide the space create a high erect vessel, soaring skywards, lit by a tower of stained-glass windows – warm colours to the north, cold ones to the south. Pierre Bergé knew the place. But what he wanted to show us seemed, at first glance, much more modest: the seats, arranged all around the altar.

Simple retractable armchairs in a slightly faded neutral beige–green, framed by wooden armrests, invited us to sit and contemplate the place. Their design was seemingly unspectacular, but it had stood the test of time. In sixty years, these chairs had not aged a bit, and that was undoubtedly what made them special. Their shape was so well designed that they remained contemporary and in good condition: timeless, and of a simplicity that is very difficult to achieve. We brought back more than we imagined from this architectural, mystical and friendly trip. We had been inspired, too, by the light and by the cork floor, which, though burnished by millions of footsteps, remained intact. And also, we discovered later, the concrete – rough, smoothed, washed and bush-hammered – which, in the sunshine and the light of the stained-glass windows, takes on ephemeral and extraordinary hues.

'And also, we discovered later, the concrete – rough, smoothed, washed and bush-hammered – which, in the sunshine and the light of the stained-glass windows, takes on ephemeral and extraordinary hues.'

– Olivier Marty

# 1,225 days to go

## The right brick

Karl Fournier's dream of a perfectly draped garment and monochrome lace gradually became an obsession. Bricks, or rather *the* perfect brick, could not be found nearby. However, the idea of looking elsewhere for a material that is so well made in Morocco seemed absurd. A brick of the colour, material and size that would be suitable for the design that Studio KO had in mind, and for the volumes that were beginning to take shape on paper, must surely exist somewhere not far from the future museum.

They just needed to find the right vein. After reviewing many samples, and visiting many brickworks, they eventually found it in among their own unlabelled boxes at the Studio KO office in Marrakech. No one knew where it came from, but it was apparently just waiting to be used.

'It was like a film. Imagine a camera suddenly coming to rest on a gold nugget that glistens in the sunlight, just long enough for you to glimpse it and for it to change the course of the narrative. It happened a bit like that', says Karl Fournier, still dazed by this stroke of luck. 'Years earlier, a landscaper from the agency had brought in some samples from a manufacturer located in Tétouan [northern Morocco], in the middle of nowhere, while we had been searching the country for the perfect material. This find was also part of the history of the project – rooted in this land, in its soil and in its traditions. It had to have the right colour, the right feel, the right surface, the right size. When you first think of a brick, you have no idea of the variety of these small blocks of earth, which all seem identical. The assurance of having finally found the right material was one of the keys to the project's success.'

'It was like a film. Imagine a camera suddenly coming to rest on a gold nugget that glistens in the sunlight, just long enough for you to glimpse it and for it to change the course of the narrative. It happened a bit like that.'

– Karl Fournier

# 1,164 days to go

## The start of the race

The first phase of a project is about imagining, dreaming, conceiving. But the transition to reality involves flowing into a very standardized process: architects go through an intense phase of drawings, technical studies, and reviews with engineers and consultants – to which regulations and constraints apply. The result must be consistent, precise, rigorous and meet the town-planning and building regulations governing the building's activity. The dream was still there, like the image of the project, which the architects never lost sight of, but the illustrations gave way to technical drawings, annotated and dimensioned.

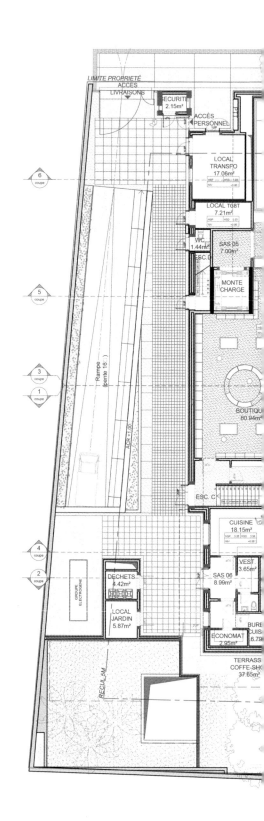

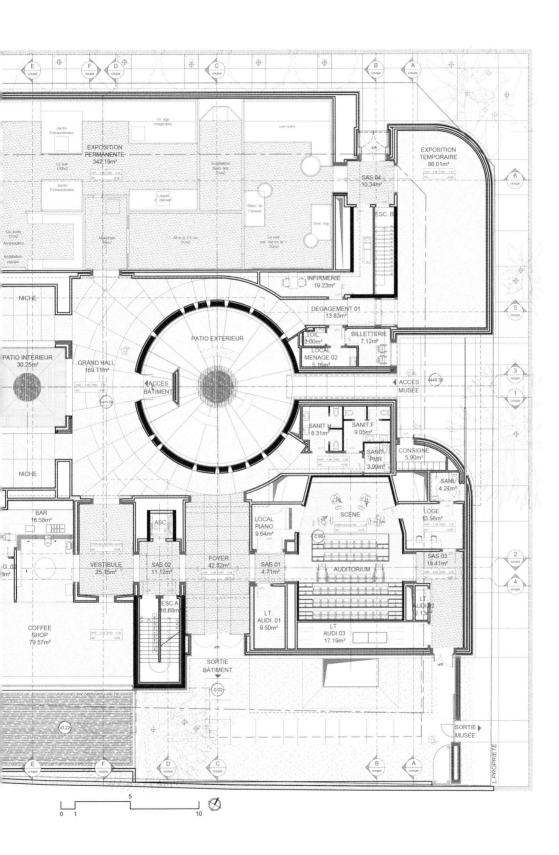

EXPOSITION
PERMANENTE
342.19m²

Jardin
Extraordinaire

Voyage
Imaginaire

Les noirs

Jardin
Extraordinaire

L'appel
d'ailleurs

SAS 04
10.34m²

ESC. B

EXPOSITION
TEMPORAIRE
86.01m²

NICHE

INFIRMERIE
19.23m²

DEGAGEMENT 01
13.83m²

PATIO EXTERIEUR

TOIL.
2.00m²

BILLETTERIE
7.12m²

PATIO INTÉRIEUR
30.25m²

GRAND HALL
169.11m²

ACCÈS
BÂTIMENT

LOCAL
MENAGE 02
5.16m²

ACCÈS
MUSÉE

SANIT.H
8.31m²

SANIT.F
9.05m²

CONSIGNE
5.90m²

NICHE

SANIT.
PMR
3.99m²

SANI.
4.27m²

BAR
16.58m²

ASC.

LOCAL
PIANO
9.64m²

SCENE

LOGE
13.56m²

VESTIBULE
25.15m²

SAS 02
11.12m²

FOYER
42.82m²

SAS 01
4.71m²

AUDITORIUM

SAS 03
18.41m²

ESC A
16.68m

LT.
AUDI 02
2.13m²

COFFEE
SHOP
79.57m²

LT.
AUDI. 01
9.50m²

LT.
AUDI.03
17.19m²

SORTIE
BÂTIMENT

SORTIE
MUSÉE

0    1          5          10

The project thus developed would require a
building permit, the mandatory 'green light'
before building work could begin. An appli-
cation for the document was filled in and sub-
mitted by Claire Patteet. Established in Rabat
since the 1970s, this Belgian architect knew
Yves Saint Laurent. A precious intermediary,
as an architect registered with the Moroccan
authorities was the essential key to starting
work, Claire Patteet took this very special
project to heart and participated in all the
weekly meetings.

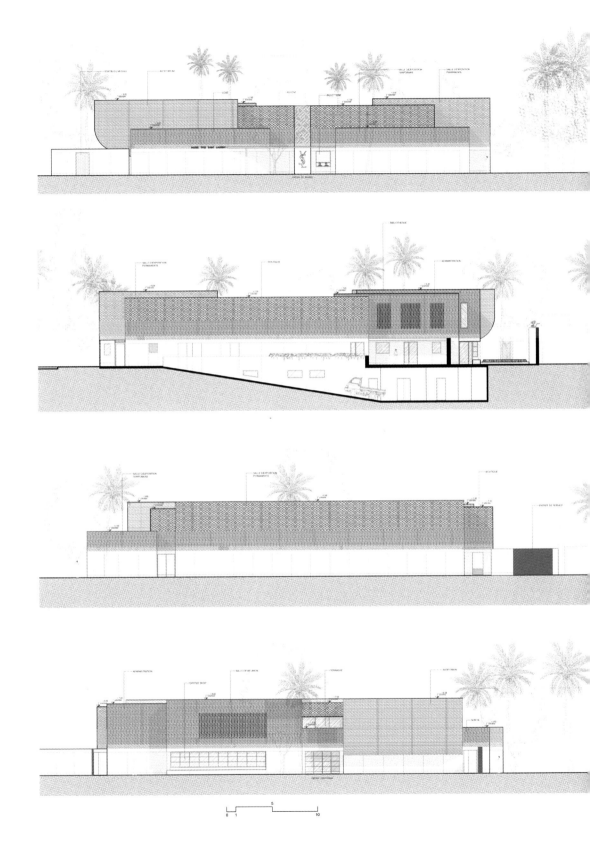

COUPE BB

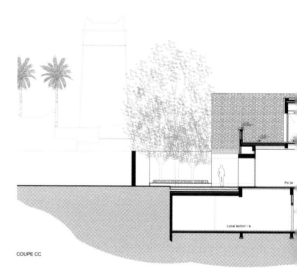

COUPE CC

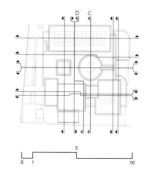

5

0  1                    10

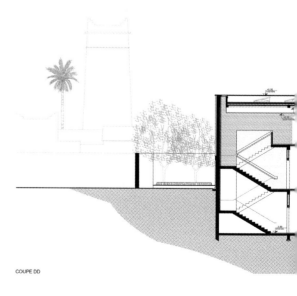

COUPE DD

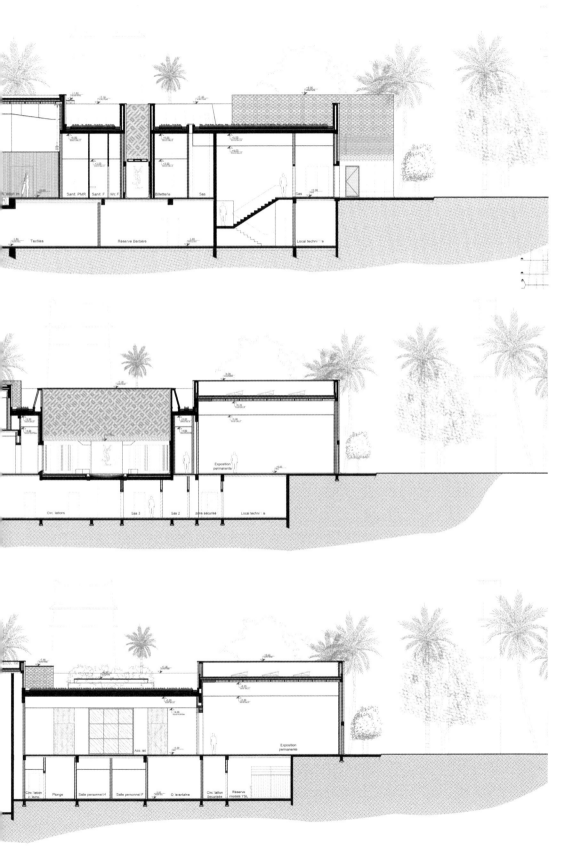

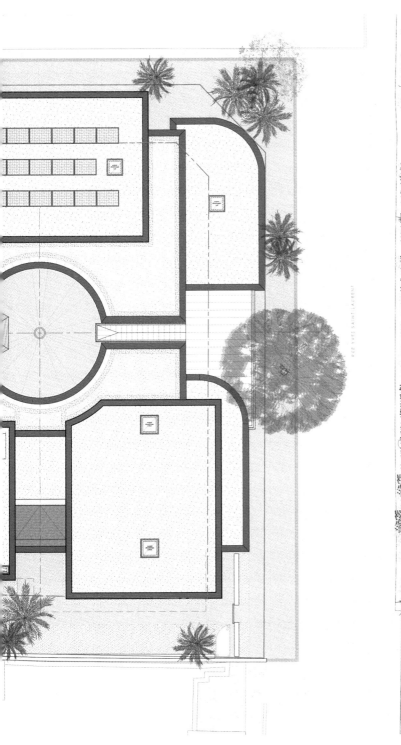

RUE YVES SAINT LAURENT

# 1,133 days to go

## The appointment
## of Björn Dahlström

'I seem to remember that Pierre Bergé simply
said: "That's good", which was a big compliment,
coming from him', reflects Björn Dahlström
A trustee of several museums and the award-
winning curator of the Luxembourg Pavilion at
the Venice Biennale, this art historian, trained
at the École du Louvre, Paris, was appointed
director of the museum in 2014, when the
building still only existed on paper.

'I seem to remember that Pierre Bergé
simply said, "That's good", which was
a big compliment, coming from him.'

– Björn Dahlström

'What was fascinating was that I participated in the project management of the museum while also being its future user', he explains, 'and I needed to learn and understand everything within a very short time frame, working with a large number of people. When I arrived, the project had already been conceived, and we then worked a lot on the cultural content. We needed to dream up events that would come to life in spaces that didn't yet exist. I learned a lot about designing a building that I usually see only once it's up and functioning. I discovered, on watching them being made, that the collection storerooms, an area that is unknown and invisible to the public, are the real nerve centre of any museum. In this case, the collection is very fragile – even more so than in other museums, because fabrics can deteriorate when in contact with the elements. We had to imagine a building capable of protecting them from humidity, harsh light and insects. Once the building was delivered, I returned to my more traditional role as a curator, organizing the day-to-day life of the museum. We have had up to 2,000 visitors per day, on average, in a space that I would have envisaged being even bigger. We needed to organize the arrival of tourists, school children and our "neighbours", who were coming to listen to a concert or attend a lecture. Reading the visitor book, it would appear that it's all worked out pretty well. Visitors leave lovely and numerous comments, on the architecture – that's what they see first – and on everything else, too. The excellence that the architects wanted to create for the setting is perfectly in keeping with the pieces on display.'

# 1,104 days to go

## White lines

Plotting the project on the ground with chalk
was a symbolic moment that was also very
moving. Such a full-scale test, using wooden
planks and lengths of string, makes it possible
to measure the space, to move from one room
to another and to check the arrangement and
the proportion of the rooms. This first encoun-
ter with reality can also reveal flaws in the
project. Will the building fit onto the plot and
will everything that has been imagined really
be possible? This very human-scale, artisanal
process – together with the small size of the
plot involved – was reminiscent of the traditional handiwork of surveyors. What could
be simpler and more conclusive than stretch-
ing ropes between stakes, scattering powder
on the ground and accurately representing
the building's boundaries in this 2,500 m²
(26,900 ft²) area? The architects also had to
imagine the height and test the setting-out
frameworks. Seeking the ultimate in purity,
they wanted only a single view from the central courtyard, a space which featured the
museum's entrance and appeared as though
dug into the volume. The sky, nothing but the
sky. No building, not even a tree or a palm
branch, should intrude into this blue circle
or disturb this very graphic arrangement. An
empty space that would keep the city and its
bustle at bay and allow visitors to enjoy the
tranquillity of the place to the full.

# 1,076 days to go

## Brainstorming in Marrakech

Messing around with ideas, or 'brainstorming',
is a key element of Studio KO's process, one
that is applied to all its major projects. On this
occasion, it gathered together the Parisian and
Moroccan teams in Marrakech for three days.
'We bring people together as a way to acceler-
ate ideas when we feel we've got a bit stuck or
simply want to enhance a project using a fresh
set of eyes. We look for them among the teams
who work with us, who know our way of doing
things really well but who find themselves
catapulted overnight into a site and a building
they don't know. It's a great way to generate
ideas that the architects of the project hadn't
thought of or, sometimes, to take us back along
avenues that we'd abandoned along the way',
explains Olivier Marty.

'It's also a moment of concentration and building together with the whole agency: Karl and Olivier are there and available, which rarely happens outside of these workshops', explains Nabil Afkiri, then director of the Morocco office. Then comes the work of assembling the essential details. The group was split into teams, with the intention of bringing together people who had not collaborated before. Some were tasked with thinking about the wall coverings, the colour, how to hide the auditorium curtain, etc. Others were responsible for discovering what sort of floor junction would be best suited to the building. There are several ways to join two surfaces together. By choosing a hollow joint in the wall or on the floor, or a covering, you can vary the feel of the spaces, the way in which the light clings to or slides across the chosen materials. 'It's also at these points of junction, friction and therefore fragility that the building suffers. The style and quality of our work is characterized by the details, and the very meticulous attention we paid to them here guarantees that the museum will age well', adds Olivier Marty. The ideas from those seventy-two hours were fed into a catalogue that became the project bible for the next two years.

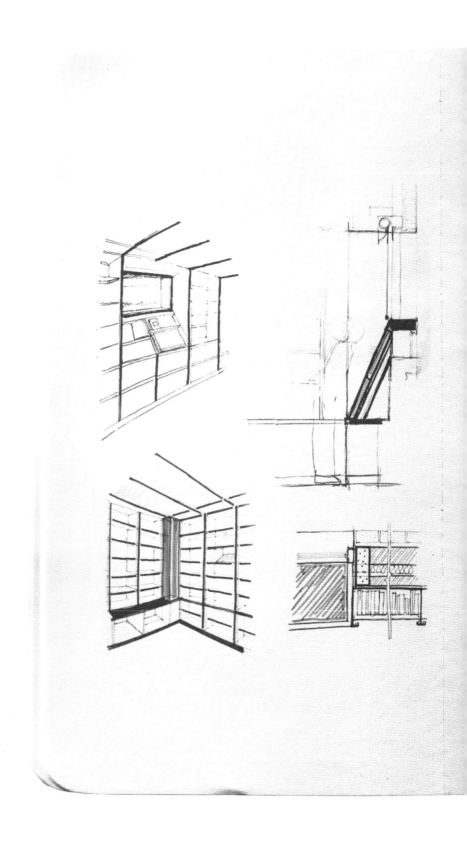

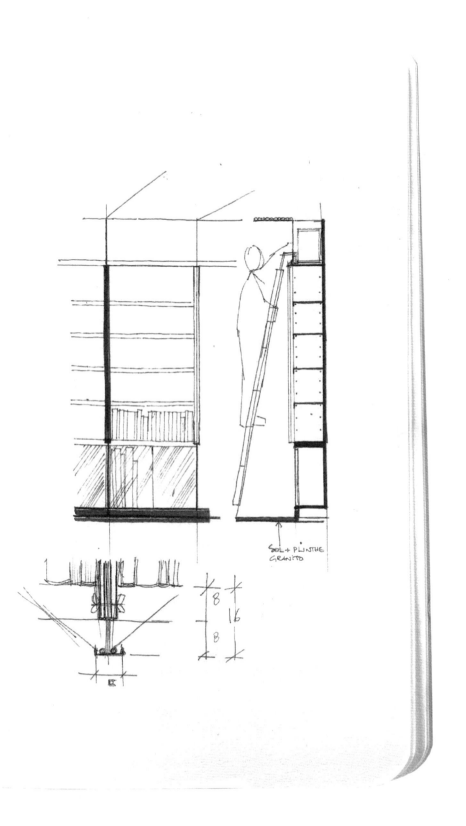

SOOL + PLINTHE
GRANITO

73

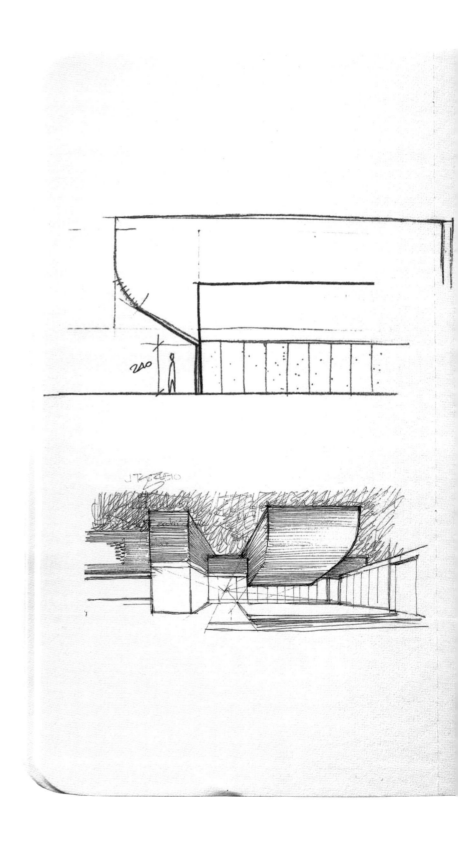

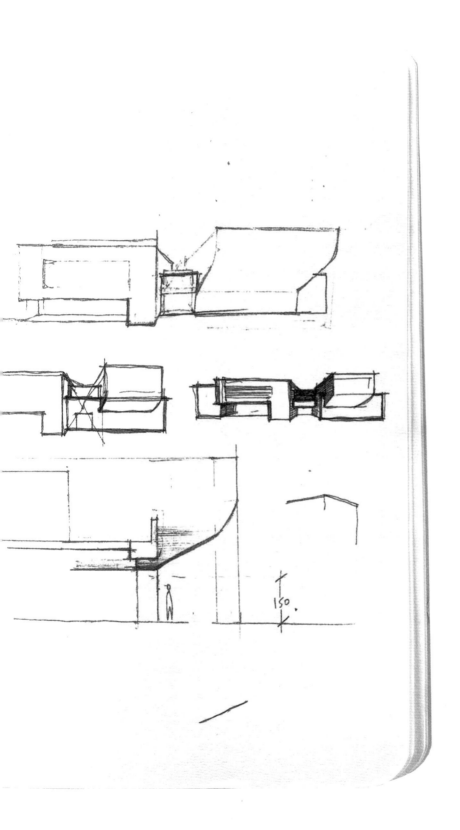

150.

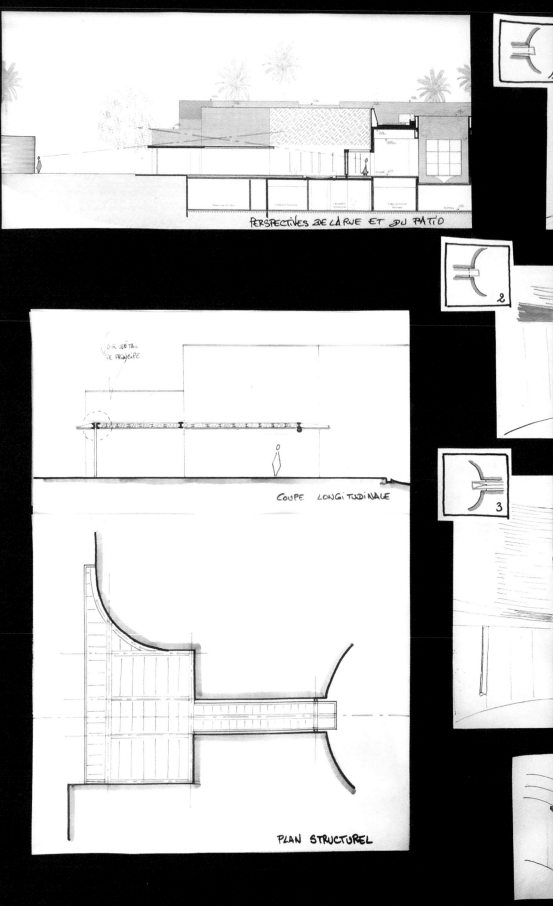

PERSPECTIVES DE LA RUE ET DU PATIO

VOIR DÉTAIL
DE PRINCIPE

COUPE LONGITUDINALE

2

3

PLAN STRUCTUREL

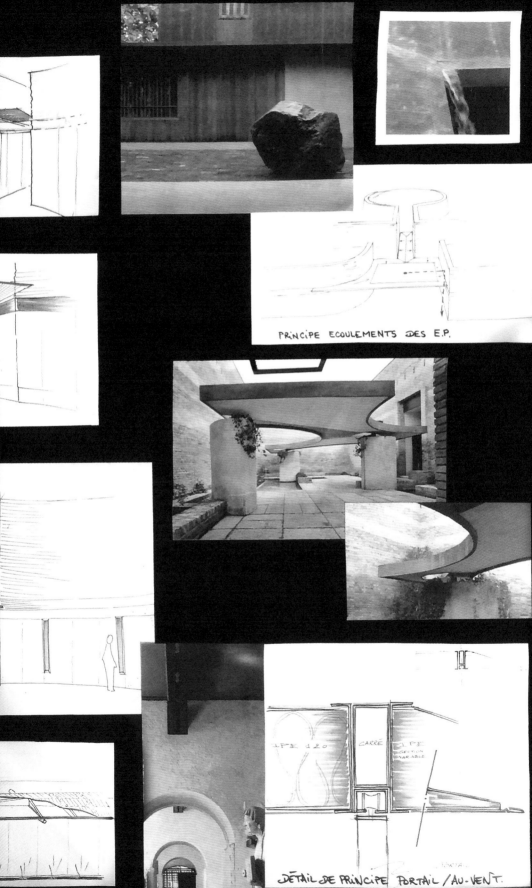

PRINCIPE ECOULEMENTS DES E.P.

DÉTAIL DE PRINCIPE PORTAIL / AU-VENT.

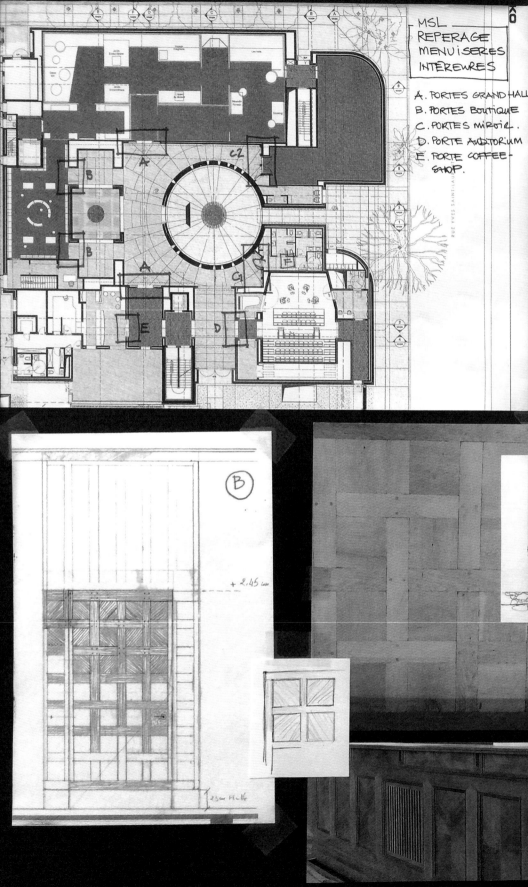

MSL
REPERAGE
MENUISERES
INTEREWRES

A. PORTES GRAND HALL
B. PORTES BOUTIQUE
C. PORTES MIROIR.
D. PORTE AUDITORIUM
E. PORTE COFFEE-
SHOP.

RUE YVES SAINT-LAURENT

+ 2,45 cm

B

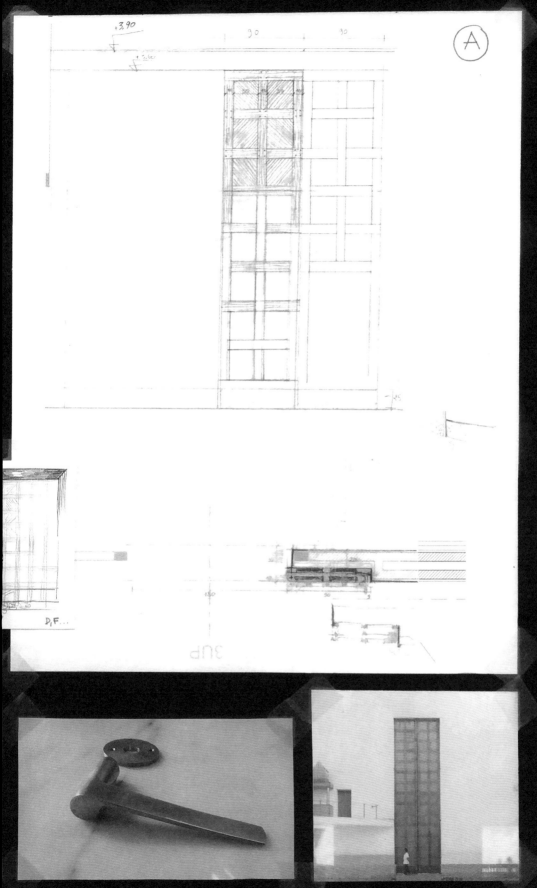

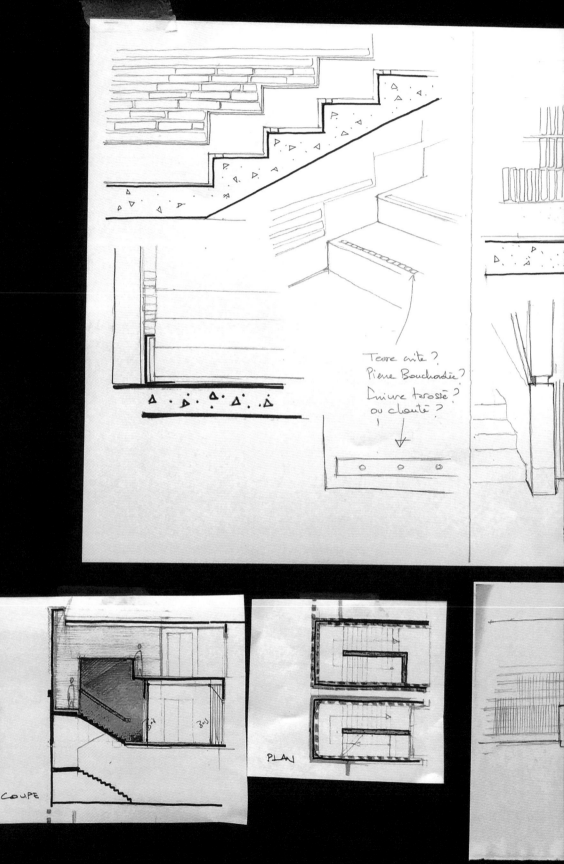

Terre cuite ?
Pierre Bouchardée ?
Cuivre terossé ?
ou chanté ?

COUPE

PLAN

 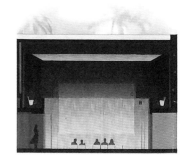

AUDIT. config CONCERT

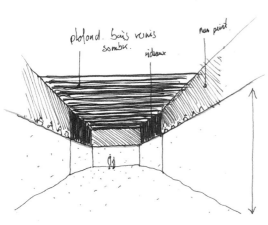

plafond. bois vernis sombre.

rideaux

non peint

rideaux vits sombre
/ bleu nuit (non).

Bois clair / cèdre vernis (lattis).

AUDIT. config projo.

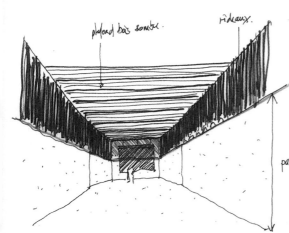

plafond bois sombre.

rideaux.

panneautage bois clair.

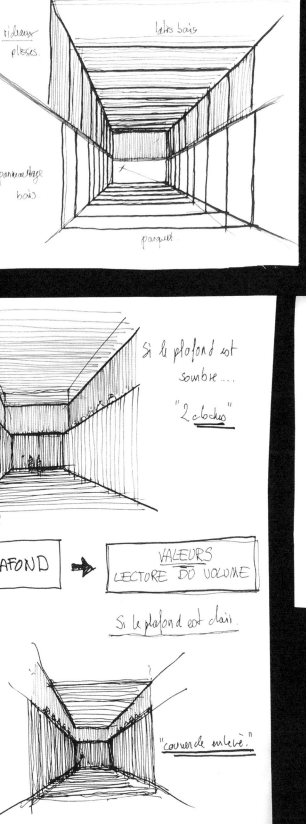

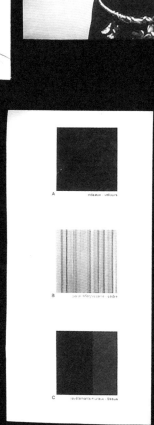

rideaux
plisses.

lattis bois

panneautage
bois

parquet.

Si le plafond est
sombre....
"2 cloches"

AFOND ➡ VALEURS
LECTURE DU VOLUME

Si le plafond est clair.

"couvercle enlevé."

A        rideaux - velours

B        paroi réfléchissante - cèdre

C        revêtements muraux - tissus

# 1,051 days to go

## An auditorium for the city

Providing a link to the present, because it hosts live events, the auditorium was part of the project from the start. Perhaps it was the part that Pierre Bergé wanted to add of himself to complement the homage being paid to Yves Saint Laurent everywhere else. In any case, it bears his name. While the other parts of the museum are built on one level, this room is suspended (both physically and symbolically), using a cantilever that extends the slope of the interior seating, as though to give this space an elevated status to those placed on the ground. The exhibition galleries naturally welcome visitors, who then discover that an entire section of the museum is dedicated to a cultural venue anchored in the present: films, opera broadcasts, symposiums and conferences are organized for our interested Marrakech 'neighbours'. The two men are no longer with us, but the two spaces are in constant dialogue. It is a way for Pierre Bergé to 'give something back' in return for what Morocco has offered him.

This variety of use required some clever planning. Being able to ensure, in the same room, good reverberation of notes during concerts, fidelity of film soundtracks, and the muted, 'dry' sound of conferences seemed contradictory. 'We worked with Findlay Ross from Theatre Projects to design this room', explains Fayçal Tiaïba. 'The project was already well under way, but he required us to "inflate" the auditorium, urging us to increase the height to the maximum for better acoustics and suggesting that we add balconies; I remember that he brought Pierre Bergé a shoebox with a model of the auditorium inside that he had made with his daughter over the weekend. It resembled a doll's house, beautiful and delicate.'

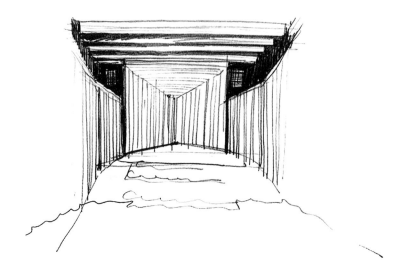

Along the lines of the Salle Cortot concert hall
of the École Normale de Musique conserva-
tory on rue Cardinet in Paris, another work
by Auguste Perret, the architects opted for a
faceted backdrop – an ideal shape to redirect
the sound. Wood dominates everywhere: on
the floor, on the walls and in slats on the ceil-
ing. A heavy velvet curtain drawn in front of
the walls allows the acoustisc of the space to be
adapted to all uses.

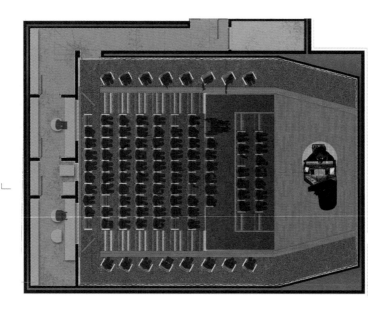

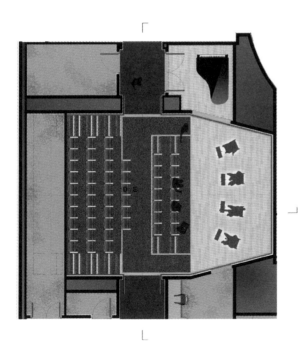

A – curtains – **velvet**

B – reflective wall – **oak**

C – wall coverings – **sculpted plaster**

D – armchair upholstery – **fabrics**

E – floor covering – **carpet**

# 1,043 days to go

## Introducing colour

It was in Marrakech that Yves Saint Laurent first discovered colour. At least, that is the legend that the people of this shimmering red-and-ochre city love to maintain. This contrasting impression needed to be echoed in the museum building: opaque yet luminous, monochrome yet colourful. 'Pierre Bergé hadn't put all that work into that famous weekend in Normandy for nothing', recalls Olivier Marty, as he relates the shock of his discovery of the Ateliers Duchemin stained-glass workshops in Paris.

It was Olivier Marty who introduced the idea of using this ancient art in the project. The inspiration for the stained-glass windows bordering the museum's central courtyard comes directly from the Église Saint-Joseph in Le Havre, whose own windows were decorated by Marguerite Huré. The architects also admired those of the Chapelle du Rosaire de Vence, on the French Riviera, designed by Matisse, which Yves Saint Laurent loved so much. In both churches, these stained-glass windows were created by the same Duchemin family. For five generations, the company has put its knowledge to work for contemporary creators. Studio KO wanted to avoid overt religious references, which could risk turning the place into a mausoleum, yet it wished to pay homage to the dazzling palette of the collections on display in the permanent exhibition gallery, a large room with black walls and floors. The architects chose large plates of tinted bubble glass 2 m (6½ ft) high, borrowing from religious buildings the principle of using warm colours to the north and cold ones to the south. The positioning of the former form a halo around the part they illuminate, the latter a rectangle drawn with extreme clarity. During the day, the windows illuminate the interior of the building, while at nightfall, these slits are most easily visible from the outside – like the facets of a lit lantern.

# 992 days to go

## A logo under the influence

'I like to grab hold of chance and take advantage of it', Philippe Apeloig explains modestly. He is the creator of the Marrakech museum's logo, which was selected from entries to a competition. There is nothing fortuitous about his design, however. 'The initials "YSL" are emblematic of Yves Saint Laurent's signature. It seemed essential to me that they appear in the logo of the museum dedicated to him. Having chosen this solution, I also used the initials of the other two words "Musée" and "Marrakech", so, the letter "M" twice. By playing on this chance element of repetition in the name of the museum, I was able to structure the graphic composition, in which two lowercase "m"s frame the three letters "YSL" in capitals. Furthermore, the rounded shapes of the two "m"s evoke the shape of the arched doors typical of Moorish architecture.'

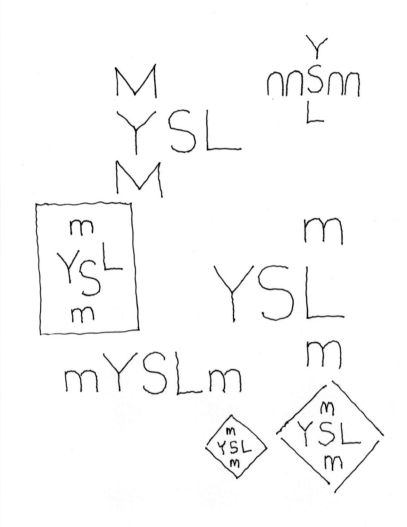

m

◆ YSL ◆

m

The geometry of the proposed design echoes the typographic structure of the famous YSL logo designed by Cassandre. The fashion designer's three initials form a small line that could evoke different shapes on a catwalk – the elongated dresses and dinner jackets created by the couturier, with their acute angles and harmonious proportions; and, in particular, the collages from which he created unique greetings cards each year. The light and the colour of the Orient, radiant and glistening, were the starting point for a range of golden and bright hues that define the museum's visual identity and are an explicit reference to the work of the French painter Yves Klein. 'Drawings are always the result of mathematical calculations', admits Philippe Apeloig. 'I found the same sense of abstraction in the work of painters who were among Yves Saint Laurent's influences.'

The whole is part of a perfect square oriented at forty-five degrees – a movement of rotation reminiscent of certain works by Mondrian and, of course, *zellij*, the enamelled terracotta tiles that adorn the walls of Arab houses.

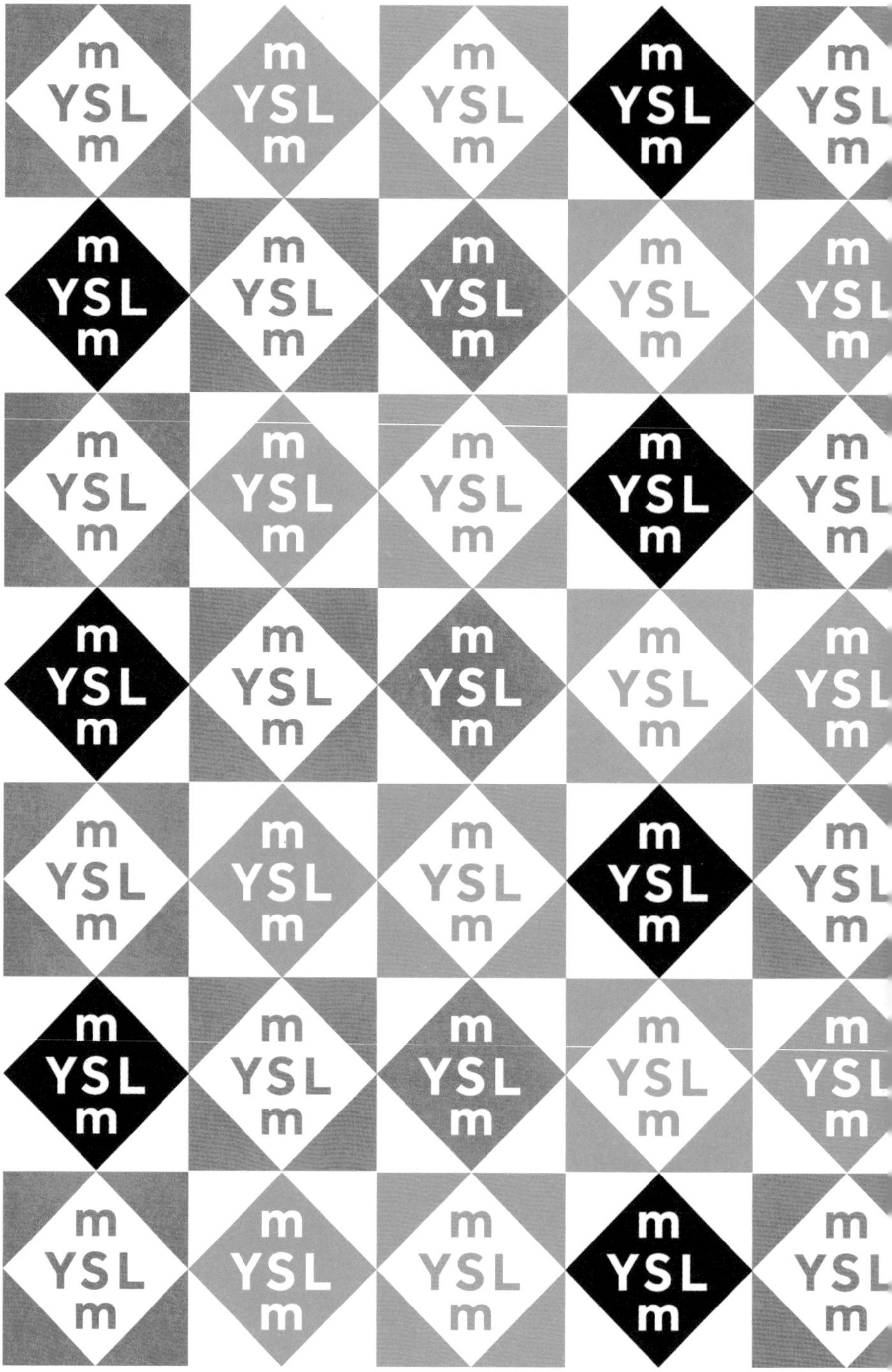
m
YSL
m

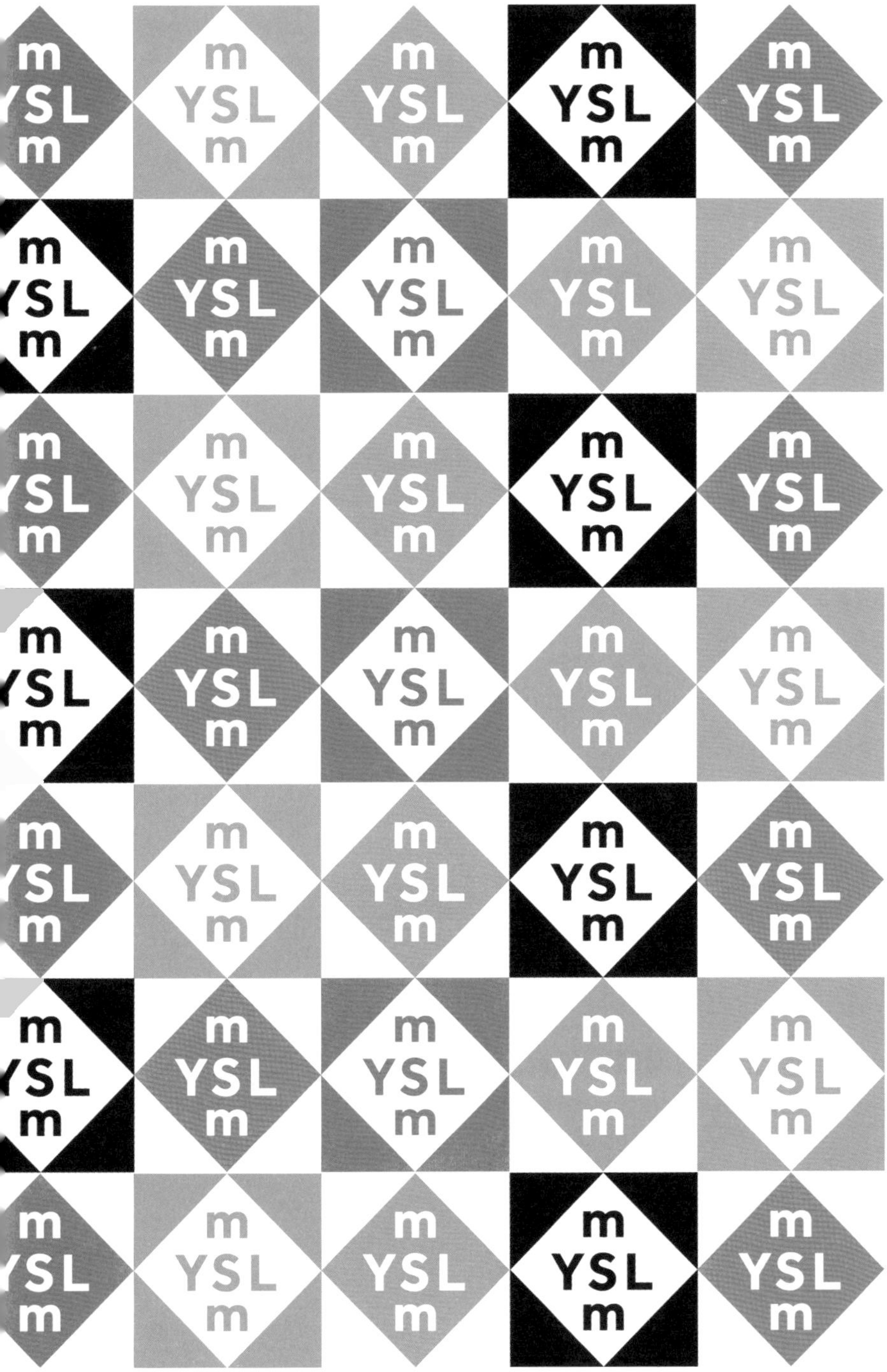
m
YSL
m

# 925 days to go

## From Tangier to
## Saint-Rémy-de-Provence

Pierre Bergé never missed an appointment. Working sessions were most often held at his home in Marrakech, but also in Saint-Rémy-de-Provence or in Tangier. But can these meetings, which took place once a month, really be called work? He always considered the project to be a family affair. And these meetings were a way of getting together in complete privacy and relaxation, always as a very small group. Under a gazebo or in his wonderful library in Tangier, under the vines of a pergola or at a cafe table in Provence, this very special client, who had worked with the top interior designers, wanted to understand everything, follow everything and see everything.

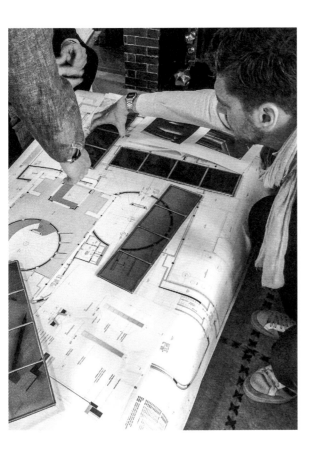

'I have very vivid memories of those moments', admits Fayçal Tiaïba. 'They're perhaps the times that marked me the most. Brilliant discussions, a passion and a joy when we unpacked the plans, when we opened our sketchbooks; a keen eye when we presented samples, materials, finishes.'

On the eve of the start of construction, the architects brought a whole series of samples. 'Pierre Bergé wanted something "made in Morocco"; it wasn't always easy to find everything there, but the architects were on the same wavelength and enjoyed the challenge', recalls Madison Cox.

# 749 days to go

## The start of building work

Pierre Bergé was there when construction began. Having converted but never built, he wanted to witness the first blows of the pickaxe that would mark the transition from dream or intellectual projection to reality. The museum was actually going to exist, and Pierre Bergé, who felt himself getting weaker, was in a hurry to see it rise from the ground.

The site was now cleared, levelled and prepared. The architects' blank page was now matched by the empty plot of land entrusted to the builders. And it was time for new people to get involved in the project. Bymaro, a subsidiary of Bouygues in Morocco, joined the team. 'They were more used to building tall towers, blocks of flats and large infrastructures. In comparison, the museum was a very small-scale thing of beauty', explains Madison Cox, 'and yet this Moroccan company fitted into the project magnificently.'

# 6 5 7 days to go

## Structural work

Beautiful proportions, fine and flexible joints, delicate limbs: the skeleton shapes the human figure. And the same is true, in a less mobile version, of buildings, too. The phases of laying the foundations and installing the structures that will define the spaces are therefore both fundamental and delicate. What is done on the inside will be seen from the outside; the structural work will determine the elegance of the finished building. The construction of the museum was subject to time constraints, an implacable countdown of milestones to which this book bears witness.

In the middle was the crane, and, all around, the building site. Things had to be done quickly from the beginning, starting by excavating the ground to anchor the elements that would rise from it. 'It became a joke: every two weeks, we would go in search of the staircase leading to the basement, which moved as the building took shape and was closed up', recalls Fayçal Tiaïba.

The structure was in reinforced concrete and, to support the roof, Bymaro chose to have the slabs prefabricated. Prestressed, they could be longer and thinner. The concrete strips were delivered and assembled on site to save time. The dismantling of the crane represented the transition to the next phase: the building was soon closed and covered. The end of this stage is traditionally celebrated with *gigot bitume* – leg of lamb cooked in asphalt – a feast provided by the roofing contractor, cooked in the same material as that used to waterproof the building. The (well-protected) leg of lamb is immersed in a bath of molten asphalt. 'One hour of cooking and the meat will be medium rare with an excellent taste', according to the recipe. Season with salt and pepper – and 'bon appétit'!

'One hour of cooking and the meat
will be medium rare with an excellent
taste', according to the recipe.

# 520 days to go

## Bush-hammered concrete

The architects imagined resting the brick facades, with their openwork and infilled sections, on a rougher and more massive structural strip – itself placed on a plinth of terrazzo.

They were not satisfied with the samples of mass-tinted concrete for the structural strip. 'We had something else in mind: Perret's exposed-aggregate concrete in Le Havre or Scarpa's Querini Stampalia Foundation in Venice; it's a very beautiful material but not sophisticated, undoubtedly a little raw, but very difficult to use. And we couldn't find it. We kept coming back to the issue of the finish of this strip, which was like a thorn in the side that you forget for a while, then the pain starts throbbing again. We would have made do, but we would have felt we were missing something', recalls Karl Fournier.

And then luck smiled upon the project. One day, Olivier Marty was filming a builder on the site crushing concrete, impressed by the strength and consistency of his handiwork. On closer inspection, the internal face of the fragments seemed to correspond to what he was looking for: an even material, but one that exposed the concrete's aggregate. 'We asked the same builder to create the entire surface of the strip around the building, in order to give it the same strength, the same handiwork and the most regular effect possible – a quality that would have been impossible to obtain using a mechanical process, which would have resulted in industrial uniformity', adds Olivier Marty.

The strip, which marks the passage from the base of the building to the much more sculpted brick, is therefore hand-finished, like a unique piece. The final proof of Pierre Bergé's conversion, at least partially, to Modernism: the monolith that stands in the circular courtyard, with its distinctive Yves Saint Laurent logo, is in bush-hammered concrete.

# 493 days to go

## The skin

A pattern, the perfection of the drape, the see-through of lace, the meticulousness of the embroidery, a garment and its lining ... The analogies are too easy, and literal comparison is often calamitous in architecture – even though the design and assembly processes are sometimes alike. A work, in both cases; a work of art more rarely. But a building is not a garment. And this one, as a tribute to Yves Saint Laurent, must serve to highlight his works while connecting, in a subtle way, the container and its contents.

With shimmering interiors, illuminated by the collections exhibited there, the museum presents plain and understated facades to those who observe it from afar. Once the brick had been chosen, conversations took place between the architect, who decided on the arrangement of bricks, and the *maalem* (bricklayer), who built the walls with extraordinary dexterity, checking the regularity of the bricklaying and the reliefs and ensuring overall harmony. On closer inspection, the bricks appear to be assembled in a meticulous and very graphic way – set back or overhanging to a greater or lesser degree, some laid at an angle – creating either a flat surface or, alternatively, a relief that is transformed by the harsh or glancing light and plays with shadows. 'This material is both very rustic and very delicate', explains Fayçal Tiaïba. 'A brick's character and colour changes as it ages, weathers, "lives". We're talking about "ghosts" that can appear when salt or saltpetre emerges from the terracotta, after the first rain.'

AURENT marrakech

'We wanted a consistent colour without it being a single swathe. Sometimes you have to let them age to see, which is why we had prototypes of the facades built', adds Fayçal Tiaïba.

Beneath the masterful brickwork, the terrazzo seems to rise from the ground with a slight curve to meet the facade walls. Although the ground is rugged, the facade is soft to the touch, revealing the aggregates that compose it: all the stones and marble are from Morocco.

The ochre-pink colour of the facade is typical of Marrakech, while the green enamelled bricks of the square courtyard recall the Palmeraie (palm grove) neighbourhood. The whole city is contained in these two shades. Here, Studio KO reinterprets *zellij*, both inside and out. The green tiles are the same as those that adorn the fireplace in Villa Léon L'Africain in Tangier, which the architects renovated for Pierre Bergé. 'It took us months to find the right colour, but he didn't want any other', recalls Olivier Marty.

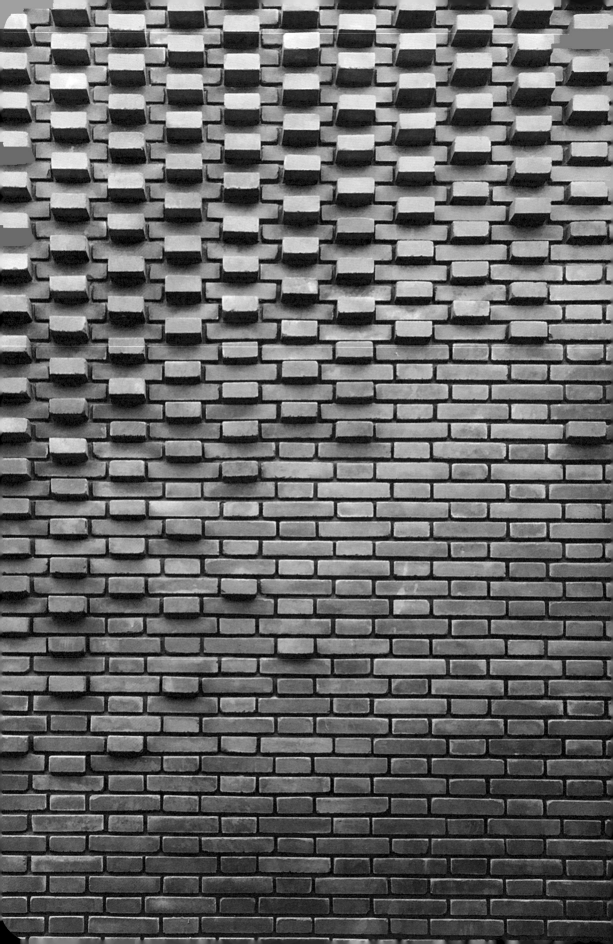

'It took us months to find the right colour, but he didn't want any other.'

– Olivier Marty

# 485 days to go

## State of siege

Is it really so hard to choose a seat? Yes, because this element of comfort and design can either make or break the reputation of a room or of even the most beautiful space. And it was particularly difficult when the seats in question were for the museum's auditorium, and when the site's owner – Pierre Bergé himself, former director of the Bastille Opera House – was involved. What came to mind was the architects' visit to the church of Le Havre and its seats designed by Auguste Perret, no less: simplicity and elegance, and still modern sixty years after their creation.

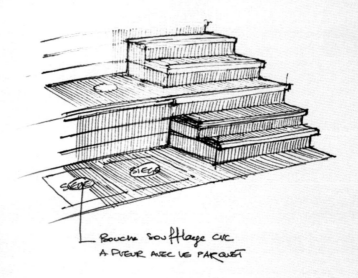

SIEG

SCENE

Bouche soufflage CVC
à fleur avec le PARQUET

ESTIMATIONS

- SOL PARQUET   SCENE / CIRCULATION / LOGE / PIANO ( LATTES 200 m
- MARCHES + CONTRE.MARCHE + NEZ   ( Marches: 250 mm long )
- PAROIS GRADING SCENE   ( Longueur:

* Réservation sous chaque siège. ( 120 mm hauteur de latte).

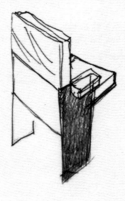

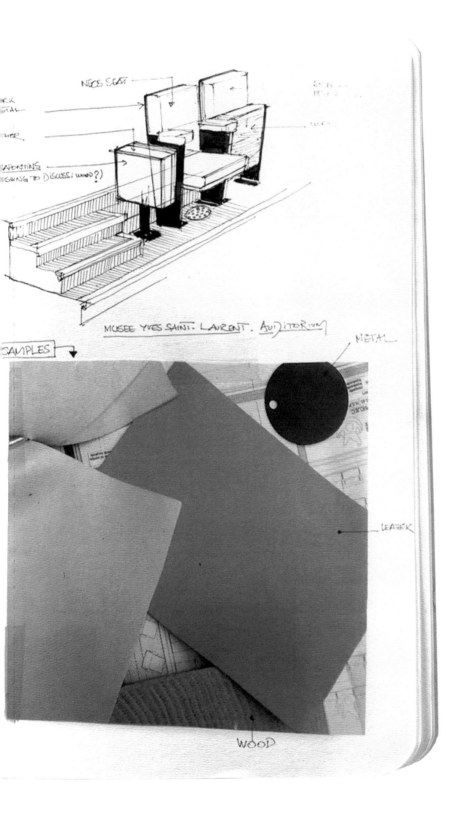

NECS SEAT

DARK
METAL

THER

...AFONTINS
...ISHING TO DISCUSS; WOOD?)

MUSEE YVES SAINT-LAURENT. AUDITORIUM

SAMPLES

METAL

LEATHER

WOOD

How could this standard be matched in the auditorium's 120 seats? Inspiration was found at Italian furniture-maker Poltrona Frau. The journey to the company's headquarters in Tolentino to try out these armchairs is one of the amusing memories the architects have of the project. 'There were four or five of us; we'd taken the plane in the morning just to go and sit down, get up, sit down again, while making our comments, and the tests lasted all day', recalls Karl Fournier, with a smile. Pierre Bergé was keen to test the comfort of the seat for himself and check that the item was perfect. 'We discovered how complicated it was to retain all the features and quality of an existing model without actually making a copy of it. Everything had to be customized: the size and resistance of the folding seat; the width of the armrests, which wear out the fastest; the firmness of the cushion – not so hard as to be uncomfortable, not so "comfortable" that it would sag – the seams, etc. Finally, it took an incredible amount of time to decide where we were going to place the little brass disc indicating the seat number', adds Karl Fournier.

# 375 days to go

## Interiors

Here, a bespoke door handle, surprisingly simple but placed on an oak marquetry surface inspired by the parquet floors at Versailles. There, a brass joint that demarcates the poured terrazzo. In the auditorium, wood is everywhere: thin slats glued together with meticulous care. The reliefs thus created sculpt the sound.

It would take an entire book to describe the attention to detail, choice of materials and surface treatments of the museum's interior. The two architects are used to building houses and hotels for clients with high standards and virtually unlimited means, enabling them to demand perfection. And it was perfection that they were pursuing in this building. Destined to welcome the public, it would be subject to tough treatment on a daily basis, but it would age well precisely because everything had been carefully designed: aesthetics, resistance and functionality. 'Although we shouldn't overdo the metaphor of clothing, the rough exterior and the very soft interior is a concept that has been carefully thought through and worked on', comments Fayçal Tiaïba. 'I really like the way in which the architects imagined the passage from the chaos of the busy street leading to the Jardin Majorelle,

to a very calm and serene world', explains Christophe Martin, the museum's scenographer, who designed the interior of the bookshop and the museography of the exhibition hall. A narrow corridor leads the visitor into the circular courtyard, where the YSL logo in brass stands out on a bush-hammered concrete surface, which the visitor has to walk around to enter the museum. The womb-like curves of the courtyard practically invite you to curl up within them. 'The route is quite intuitive', adds Christophe Martin, 'visitors often start with the temporary exhibition gallery, which is arranged symmetrically with the auditorium, then enter the darkness of the permanent exhibition hall, the second door of which opens directly into the shop. They can thus continue their museum visit in Saint Laurent's world, as I was inspired by his first Rive Gauche boutique on rue de Tournon.'

# 322 days to go

## Well-conserved collections

Inside the building and under the watchful and cautious eye of Véronique Monnier, consultant in preventive conservation, another invisible museum evolved – a 700 m² (7,535 ft²) shelter buried underground, housing the nerve centre of the museum: the collection storerooms. The basement space houses works in a protected environment, where compliance with conservation norms is a prerequisite for loans granted by the foundation in Paris and other organizations.

The precious works displayed in the exhibitions are stored here (along with collections belonging to the Berber Museum, added later, for which space was found through efficient planning). Every week, one or two designs are exchanged; every two months, all the mannequins are redressed – ensuring the constant rotation of this mini collection of 250 pieces, a small part of the foundation's total, which contains more than 5,000 pieces in Paris.

Dresses, jackets, skirts and other items regularly pay a visit to the restoration workshops. Handling them requires laboratory-level precautions: air purity and the stability of humidity levels are checked regularly and are regulated by precision climate cabinets. The conservation areas are thermally insulated and protected from dust and natural light, which could alter colours and fabrics. Outfits returned from the exhibition halls are quarantined, disinfected and sometimes vacuum-packed or frozen before being stored, to prevent insects nesting in them and wreaking havoc in the darkness of wardrobes or drawers. Mobile cabinets on rails were made to measure. The works are catalogued and stored in them flat, without tension or folding. Clothing, shoes, hats: every item has its place. There are also rooms for studying collections (stocktaking, photographing, tagging) and for preparing them for exhibitions; the pieces need to be adjusted on the mannequins. A goods lift connects the basement to the museum and is used exclusively for the collections in order to avoid any risk of contamination.

Travée 1

Fond
48A
48B
48C
49A
49B
49C
50A
50B
50C
51A
51B
51C

# 210 days to go

## Final adjustments

Lighting, sound … it was the moment of truth, when reality hit home. Acoustics, reverberations and the subtlety of the nuances all needed to be tested in the museum. Although the position of the lights and the orientation of certain panels to vary the feedback and alleviate echoes could still be adjusted, there was no longer time to modify either the spaces or the entryways.

'We were about to launch the ship, hoping it wouldn't sink', says Fayçal Tiaïba with a smile. 'We were checking to ensure that everything we'd imagined in drawings and models worked as well in reality.' That day in March 2017, it was all hands on deck: Akari-Lisa Ishii, the lighting designer who had imagined how the volumes would be sculpted by light; Victoria Chavez, Theatre Projects' acoustical engineer, without whom an auditorium is just another room; and Bymaro's engineers, who were responsible for temperature control and air circulation. Sight, sound, thermal and physical comfort: each sense needed to be gratified and protected from any irritation that might distract or spoil the pleasure of the viewer or listener. These tests were also a chance to discover any unforeseen eventualities. The surprises were mostly good ones – particularly, the exterior in the daytime, the interior at night and moving from one to the other as the light fades, when the museum is lit only by the stained-glass windows of the circular courtyard. 'We had planned to have exterior lighting but we abandoned it, which was no bad thing', notes Olivier Marty. 'Lighting a building at night is ecologically and economically questionable. Why do it, except for aesthetic reasons? In the end, it's only the YSL logo, engraved in the concrete, that emerges, dramatically lit, from the circle of the main courtyard.'

'We were about to launch the ship, hoping it wouldn't sink.'

– Fayçal Tiaïba

# 155 days to go

## Alone on stage

The first and last time that Pierre Bergé would see the museum completed was on the 19 May 2017. He came especially for the acceptance of the building. This technical milestone, a compulsory stage in any construction, is always a symbolic occasion, marking the handover of the premises. All the teams remember this event as an emotional moment, one that was made even more solemn by an involuntary setting: the auditorium lighting was being adjusted, and only the room and the audience were lit while the stage remained in darkness.

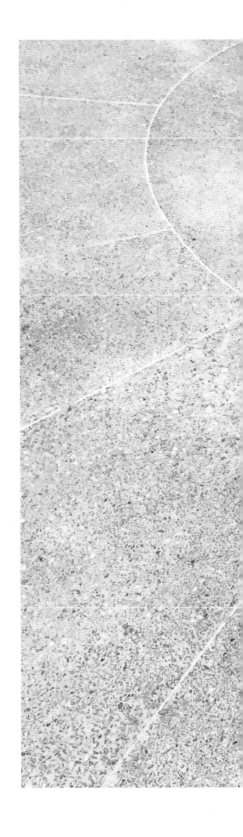

Some protective plastic sheeting still lurked at the edge of the stage like tissue paper from a partially unwrapped gift. Pierre Bergé was alone on stage, seated in the dark. He warmly thanked all those involved: Madison Cox, the foundation's president; Björn Dahlström, the director of the museum; the architects; and the teams who had worked on its construction.

'It's not just the artists' work, you have to support and understand them, and I know something about that', he added. He announced what was to follow: the planned opening and how he had imagined it down to the finest detail – 'something very lively'. The date of 14 October 2017 had been booked for ages as the only time slot available in the diary of violinist Renaud Capuçon, whom Pierre Bergé wanted to hear play. From where he sat, he looked around the room for the first time with its chairs and the audience, and smiled. 'It's not very big, this room, but it's quite something. I wanted this great and fine project to be not only a museum but also a cultural centre, because lectures and music are important and that's what we're going to do here.'

# 142 days to go

## Landscaping

Next to the Jardin Majorelle, the museum deliberately displays an almost austere restraint. The two places complement each other: a lush natural space in which stands a workshop that has become the Berber Museum, and a monolithic and monochrome block enlivened with a few touches of green. Madison Cox, who had previously brought the Jardin Majorelle back to life, worked with the very graphic nature of the museum's brick facades and chose plants that would respect the building's architectural style without spreading and overwhelming it. There are no vines, no climbers, no flowers that would vary the landscape or colours from one season to another. The original design of the land-scaping will change little over time – except in the square courtyard, where a few lianas are allowed to wind their way as they please.

As the building occupies almost the entire plot of land, there are few spaces for plants. The landscaper had to limit himself to three islands: the square courtyard, the cafe terrace surrounding the water feature, and the museum exit. 'We first imagined planting the courtyard with palm trees, as a reminder of the palm grove at the origin of the city', explains Karl Fournier. In the end, given the absence of a sufficient layer of soil, only the perimeter was planted. 'I chose aloe vera, which is very pointed and, like the building, has a strong outline', explains Madison Cox, who cites French painter 'Le Douanier' Rousseau's lines and clean, clearly defined shapes as a source of inspiration. He also planted prickly pears, which are typically Moroccan but paradoxically scarce in the Jardin Majorelle. These cacti, with stems widening into large discs, provide additional shapes and a series of shades of green that blend into a single hue, in the same way that the bricks of the facades, despite all being different, create a single ochre.

# 131 days to go

## Press conference

'In 2002, I decided to turn memories into projects. To do that, you have to have memories', Pierre Bergé declared, using the French word *souvenirs,* in both its senses – memories and keepsakes ('things'). 'Some 5,000 garments and more than 200,000 sketches, drawings, objects: that's a lot of "uncountable things"', he said in June 2017 during the launch conference for the two new Yves Saint Laurent museums, in Paris and Marrakech. He was no doubt including in this inventory moments and images that these two symbolic places implicitly held for him.

'We discovered Marrakech in 1966 and it really was love at first sight', he added. Indeed, the discovery was so special that the art lover and the fashion designer were inspired to choose the Moroccan city as their second home, first renovating a house there and soon afterwards saving the Jardin Majorelle, which was in a pitiful state and threatened with extinction in the 1980s. Forty years later, Pierre Bergé had a building constructed right next to it, no doubt destined for the same bright future: 'I had dreamt of top international architects, but then I said to myself, why put yourself to that trouble?' It was easier to simply pick up the phone and call ones he knew, with whom he was already in contact.

Understandably moved, the two partners of Studio KO explained to the audience their creative process: one dreaming, the other drawing. 'The idea of an opaque building came to me very quickly – to protect the collections and because Moroccan houses face inwards', said Karl Fournier. Olivier Marty expressed himself using lines, volumes, colours: 'Little by little, shapes and, for the first time in our work, curves appeared. Usually, our angles are sharp. I interpreted them in plan and in elevation like the upstroke of handwriting or the fall of a fabric.'

On the screen, a few rare photographs showed the building. Björn Dahlström explained the different spaces: the exhibition hall; the auditorium, revealed for the first time; the bookshop; the cafe; the collection storerooms; and the themes – masculine–feminine, Africa, imaginary voyages and extraordinary gardens. The teaser was perfect: the audience would have to visit and see for themselves.

'In 2002, I decided to turn memories
into projects. To do that, you have
to have memories.'

– Pierre Bergé

# 60 days to go

## At the heart of the museum, the collection

On leaving the museum, most visitors are very impressed by the collections they have just admired. The attention to detail, the harmony of the shapes, the brilliant and bold mix of colours, the purity of the design: everything about Yves Saint Laurent is powerfully summed up here. Would he have been surprised to learn that it took two years to select the pieces that would form this exceptional collection – two years to assemble the 200 outfits that, since the museum's opening, have been displayed so successfully in the large black nave of the permanent exhibition hall?

'I'm particularly moved when I see my clothes. The jumpsuits, the dinner jackets, everything that I used to wear, that I love more than anything. It's a second skin for me.'

– Betty Catroux

'While Dominique Deroche [who worked for Yves Saint Laurent for more than 40 years] and Pierre Bergé "dressed" the mannequins, Christophe Martin, a worthy disciple of Bob Wilson [stage director], pared down the stage, stripped away the decor and perfected the lighting so that it illuminated these weightless yet very present contours', recalls Björn Dahlström. These clothes tell stories, travel inspirations that speak of different regions – evoking them lightly and unexpectedly, never literally. There are a few recurring pieces: it is impossible to imagine a Yves Saint Laurent collection without a dinner jacket. Pierre Bergé wanted sparkle, evening dresses, something spectacular. More than 1,000 items loaned by the Pierre Bergé–Yves Saint Laurent Foundation in Paris made the journey from Paris to Marrakech in an articulated lorry accompanied by the director, who was no doubt in a hurry to arrive and get this precious cargo safely stored.

The pieces are exhibited for a few months and are then returned to the collection storerooms created especially for them, where they are stored, protected and sheltered from light, heat, insects and other intruders. The storerooms of the small museum are among the safest in all of Africa.

# 39 days to go

## Pierre Bergé is gone

Pierre Bergé passed away at Mas Théo, his house in Saint-Rémy-de-Provence, on 8 September 2017, a few weeks before the official opening of the museum, four years after he had dreamed of it. Illness had tired him, then weakened him, forced him to remain seated and then lying down while the building was rising up, tall and strong. 'We'd seen him in July, and shared a musical moment with him under the pergola, as we often did: Schubert's "Trio Opus 100" and a Mahler symphony', recall the two Studio KO partners. 'The next day, we said goodbye to him; he replied: "Adieu"…'

•

# 1 day to go

## The Senufo bird

The one that remained, and will remain: a large sculpture acquired in 1960 from the art dealer Charles Ratton was the only piece saved from the auction following Yves Saint Laurent's passing. Of a long wooden hornbill, the primordial bird and protector of the Senufo people of the Ivory Coast, its swollen belly makes it a symbol of fecundity and fertility, and it represents and evokes prosperity. Perhaps Pierre Bergé and Yves Saint Laurent had chosen it as an omen or a token of good fortune when they were starting their incredible collection. And perhaps it was for this reason that Pierre Bergé had decided to keep it as his only memento. As he used to say, 'It was Duchamp who taught us – what I'm going to say shocks a lot of people – that what is most important in art isn't always the result but the artistic gesture. And the artistic gesture of an African sculpting this truly admirable thing is ultimately as important as that of Brancusi. The result, in a way, is the same: it's just as beautiful; the emotion it arouses is just as great.'

As Karl Fournier described it nicely, 'It wasn't planned; it just happened during the project, as though the bird had landed there, as though it had completed its journey in this place that reunites these two men.'

# Launch Day

## Inauguration

The date had been set for a long time, and everyone had replied in the affirmative to Pierre Bergé's invitation to come and celebrate Yves Saint Laurent's work. Strangers and celebrities, close friends and casual visitors, Marrakshis and tourists. The emotion was palpable, and the names of the two men were on everyone's lips. Yves Saint Laurent, Pierre Bergé. The two-headed eagle. All the famous people who had supported the two men in their crazy adventure were there: Betty Catroux, Catherine Deneuve, Marisa Berenson. Princess Lalla Salma was also present. Did she come out of friendship for Pierre Bergé, with whom she used to take tea in the Jardin Majorelle from time to time? In any event, her presence did a great deal to draw public attention to this Moroccan museum. 'On the international scene and in the fashion world, it didn't need publicity; it was already being talked about', says Madison Cox. 'By contrast, all the newspapers and radio and television broadcasts that talked about the event brought it into the homes of people who, without that media attention, would doubtless never have heard of it. I'm sure that Pierre Bergé would have been extremely proud and happy; he wanted to put Morocco in the spotlight.'

'It was a chance for many Marrakshis
and inhabitants of other Moroccan
cities to discover the influence that
their country had had on Yves Saint
Laurent and on his work, and they felt
a great sense of pride.'

– Madison Cox

The whole city was flying Yves Saint Laurent's flag. The Stade de France fashion show was projected in Jemaa el-Fna square. The band Mashrou' Leila performed at the Theatro club. As a finale, Renaud Capuçon gave a violin recital in the auditorium – where he promised himself he would record an album, so impressed was he with its acoustics. But beyond the media-friendly society event, beyond the party and official dinners, Pierre Bergé was giving a final message of farewell and thanks. He was there, in the midst of the crowd gathered by and for him. For Studio KO, it was a unique moment: the ideal opportunity to gather together the three offices – Marrakech, Paris, London – for the first time.

The employees met up with much joy and not a little relief, too. It was a chance for some of them to finally meet, and for others to discover Marrakech. And a chance for Karl Fournier and Olivier Marty to look back over the road they had travelled, not only to complete the museum but also to create such a large 'family'.

'I feel very moved. I think I'll have to come back in the daytime, when it's calmer. But they've understood everything; it's wonderful.'

– Catherine Deneuve

# Studio KO

**Catherine Sabbah: How does the Yves Saint Laurent museum stand out from your usual work?**

Olivier Marty: Above all, it marked a transition to another age, a first form of maturity. It's in keeping, if not with our work – in certain aspects, it represents a departure – at least with our approach to architecture and our way of practising it.

Karl Fournier: What was really groundbreaking was the building type, which we were tackling for the first time: our practice entails finding a specific response to each new problem, so the solution here was inevitably going to be different, at least in terms of its form. The continuity with our previous work was that here again we were trying to rid ourselves of any stylistic temptation, any stumbling over our own grammar.

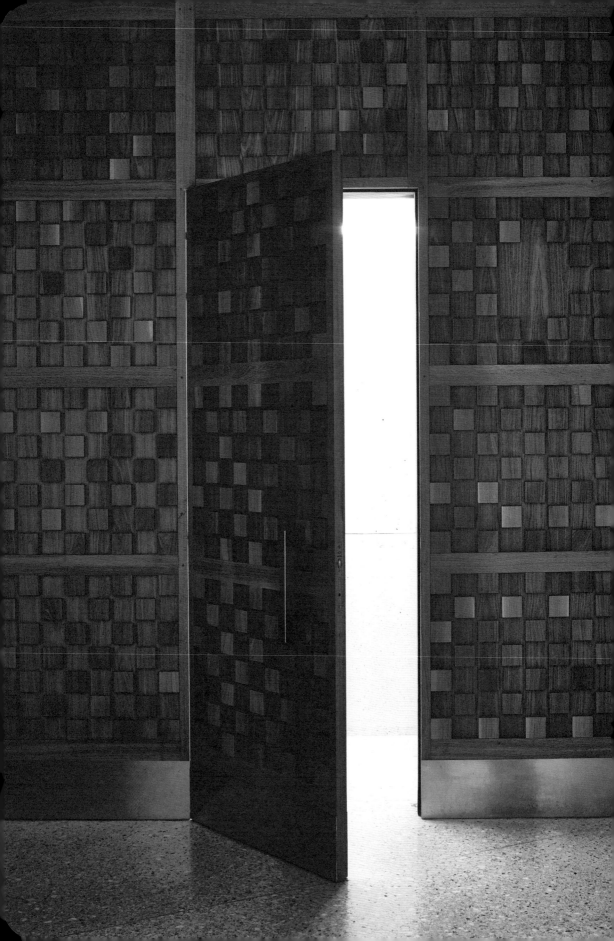

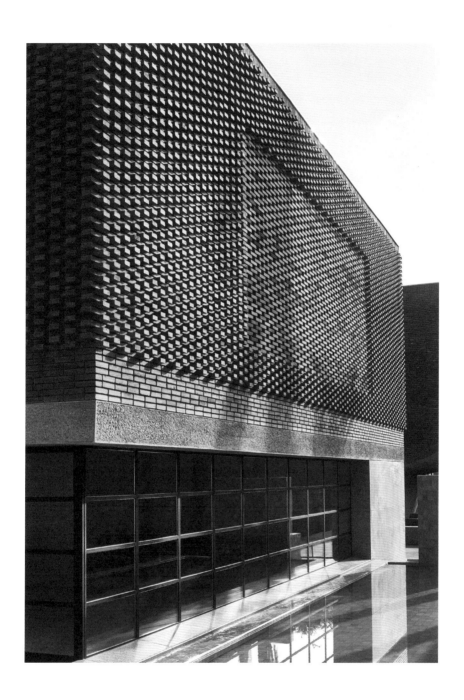

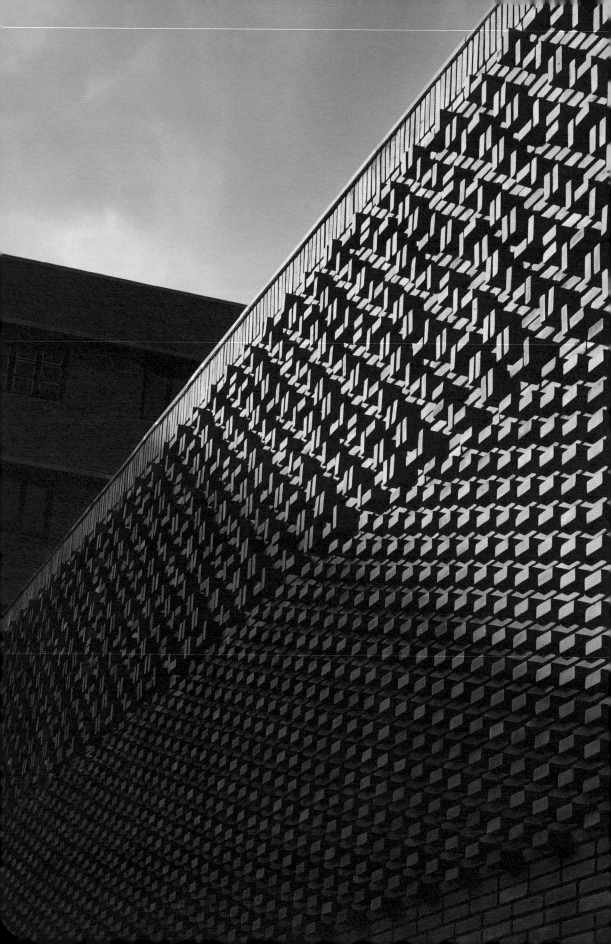

**Did this commission for a public building give you greater responsibilities towards its visitors and the place where it's located?**

OM: When we design a project, the issues of legacy and of history are very present. This entails a responsibility towards people and the landscape. When we're building on a natural site, with no other buildings around, we probably feel this responsibility even more acutely than we do in a city, where the question of integration into the context is more social, human, common. Our responsibility towards Yves Saint Laurent and the community interested in his work, in fashion and in culture in general, was very important, because it has an effect on the collective imagination of hundreds of thousands of people. And that, in truth, is a staggering thought!

KF: Our first responsibility was towards Pierre Bergé. We wanted both to show ourselves worthy of his absolute trust and to reconcile him to contemporary architecture. To make him proud of the only from-scratch building project he'd ever instigated – and that would be his last. We also had the responsibility of bringing him the joy and satisfaction, during the last three years of his life, of seeing his dream come true. It was also an enormous pressure on us to have our name associated with such a phenomenal fashion designer, not to mention the certainty of being exposed, judged and observed. There was no room for mistakes or mediocrity.

**Given its size, its content and the tribute it represents, has this museum shifted your perception of architecture?**

KF: In terms of its size, no, because we've been used to designing much larger buildings and projects. But in terms of its meaning and what it represents, yes, without a doubt. I've been struck by reading and hearing the positive comments it's inspired: many people have been very moved by the architecture. No doubt because of its very human scale and its simplicity. In that sense, yes, it's changed my perception of architecture; even the simple fact of it being designed for the public completely turned our perspective upside down.

OM: Yes, we realized that there was no need to be ostentatious with this building or for it to be immense in order for it to leave a positive impression on people. It's actually modest in its almost domestic size. It doesn't overpower the visitor and doesn't try to impress, and that's perhaps the reason it moves people.

**You drew curves while you usually draw only angles; why this formal 'softening'?**

OM: We were probably ripe for introducing new forms. It seemed obvious to us that not wanting to paraphrase the fashion designer, one of the ways to pay tribute to him was to develop its plan as volumes, a bit like a garment. It was the moment to be bold.

KF: While visiting the foundation's archives, we were struck by these drawings of patterns that were like real architecture. It's important to be sincere, and that inspired us; we said to ourselves, this is a way to start the dialogue with the designer without getting too much into direct reference. It was also a way to be freer, more abstract. Using a perfect cylinder in architecture is not that common, unless you're designing a grain silo.

Until then, we'd been more restrained because we're not looking for technical prowess. Our buildings are simple and very anchored; here, we just tried to rise a little without succumbing to the prevailing madness.

**What architectural differences are entailed in the transition from private to public use?**

OM: It's very odd, because the building isn't aimed at anyone in particular. And that offers greater freedom. It's important to us that our clients are happy with the projects we create for them, but here we were obliged to free ourselves from that desire to please the client. It shifts the subject, who is no longer the client – their life, their tastes, their expectations, their obsessions – but a multitude of people we don't know. From then on, we're automatically freed from this constraint of designing for someone. It's no longer a dedication to one person.

KF: This was the first time we'd designed a place that would feature on a city postcard and would quickly become one of its emblematic sites. Our private projects are, by definition, private, sometimes even excessively so, and arouse the interest only of our employees and those close to us, but, in the case of the Yves Saint Laurent Museum, we knew from the outset that there was an expectation and we wanted the building to occupy a special place in the life of this city and in popular imagination.

Also, and more prosaically, when it comes to tackling a building open to the public, there are a whole series of standards and regulations that need to be complied with, some of which are utterly ridiculous. It becomes a power struggle between very unequal forces: on one side, the champions of the beautiful and the free – in other words, the madmen – and on the other, the upholders of law enforcement, that is to say the knowledgeable, the sententious – the normal people.

We were not at all prepared for this shock, for this systematic negation of any attempt – however small, however fragile – to create poetry.

How would you describe the influence of this very particular content (the collections, the presence of Yves Saint Laurent) on your design and the way you conceived this project?

OM: A museum containing a collection of clothing and accessories was a godsend because textiles need to be totally protected from natural light, both for exhibitions and for conservation. From then on, all that remained was the task of composing the volumes, of linking the functions of the project, of progression and of fluidity. So, we were given the opportunity to design a building that, from its exterior facades, is very mysterious, which is the dream of any architect – or at least was ours. A minimum of windows to create – what freedom!

KF: Yes, it's true – but, paradoxically, when you enter, it's bathed in light and the visitor route is never in darkness. Here, I've just remembered something funny: when I was a student, I designed a museum that was totally opaque on the outside and with no artificial light. We distributed torches at the entrance and everyone made their own light.

Right from the start, we had the idea of a building like a garment and its lining; as smooth on the inside as it is rough on the outside. We wanted its outer skin to act as a protection against the bustle of the city.

You chose materials that you could source very locally. Was that the decision of the client, who wanted a Moroccan building? Or was it a principle of sustainable development and respect for what was already there?

KF: In our practice, it's a foregone conclusion that we work as much as possible with what we can find locally – materials and techniques. And that was one of the things that had impressed Pierre Bergé when we'd invited him to come and visit one of our sites many years before he offered us this project. We used to have passionate conversations with him about contemporary art and contemporary architecture. We didn't agree – he used to tease us a lot – but on this subject, we were of one mind. It was something that was obvious, dictated both by concern for the environment and by a deep respect for the place that was hosting us, in all its aspects – geographical, human, cultural and architectural.

OM: However, using local materials didn't prevent us from seeking to create a tension between the building and its environment. In fact, the museum was derived from two movements: that of fusion with the ochre city, in terms of its colour and its material, mainly terracotta, and of tribute to it in the use of brick and its Islamic aspect. And the tension created by its opacity, its volumes and its relationship to the street – it has freed itself completely of the codes of the surrounding residential area.

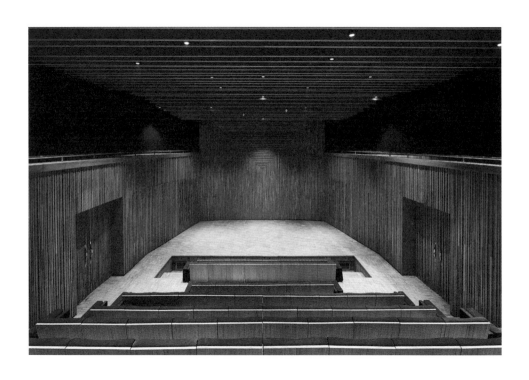

'We try to remain open to suggestions from everyone, to let people speak and share their ideas ... We're not designing alone in our ivory tower; we feel supported, enriched by the work of each person.'

– Karl Fournier

Your work as architects is very complete in the sense that it takes into account every aspect of the building, from its surroundings to the smallest interior details. How do you choose to equip yourselves in order to be able to handle the architecture, design and decoration, from conception to realization?

OM: Sometimes, we realize, with a tinge of regret, that our projects are developed in a fairly top-down fashion: the initial idea that comes from the two of us is like an essence, a concentrate that needs to be developed without ever losing its strength and singularity; at the same time, the employees who worked on the project all felt involved and that they had something to offer. Architects, interior designers, drafters and decorators all have elements of the museum somewhere that have come from their hand, their reflections and their work. So, many feel that the project is also theirs. And this is true as much of the project manager as of the person who sketched the first brick in a notebook.

KF: On many of our projects, we organize off-subject work sessions with members of the studio. These sessions are enriched by each person's fresh outlook, their experience and their expertise relating to one aspect of the project or another. We try to remain open to suggestions from everyone, to let people speak and share their ideas. It's like the genie in Aladdin's lamp, who emerges when there's friction. We're not designing alone in our ivory tower; we feel supported, enriched by the work of each person. Building demands considerable energy, which can only come out of a collective effort. It's then up to us to channel it.

It's a great asset for us to have, within the agency, talented people as diverse as architects with an engineering background, stylists with an artistic sensibility and people trained in interior decoration. We're fortunate to have people with very different profiles, from diverse backgrounds and with varied experiences, working together – and for us, it was intuitive and obvious to work like this.

**Did this experience make you want to scale up?**

OM: Yes and no. Bigger, but only provided that things like the time spent drawing, questioning, designing and focusing on details remain of the same quality.

KF: Yes and no, too. No, because large scale is dangerous. The bigger the project, and the more people there are involved in the building process, the further away the architect can get from it, and the greater the risk of them being dispossessed of it. Yes, because there lies within every architect, whether consciously or more deeply hidden, a megalomaniac. We imagine for a moment that we can do anything, design anything; we're constantly pushing ourselves to the limit. But the advantage of working as a duo is that you can always rely on the other one to bring you back down to earth.

# Image captions

**Based on an original idea
by PIERRE BERGÉ**

The contracting authority was Jardin Majorelle SCA, which delegated on-site management to Madison Cox and Björn Dahlström.

Along with Pierre Bergé, they entrusted the architectural design to:

– Studio KO: Karl Fournier and Olivier Marty

– Fayçal Tiaïba was the project manager

Supported by Elena Jiménez, Mohamed Rabia Akhal Laayoune, Marouane Bendahmane, Yassir Lemdihb and Hervé Micaud

**Project management**

- Chief architect and design of the collection storerooms: Jean-Michel Rousseau Architectes; project manager: Reda Issolah

- Project architect: Claire Patteet

- Landscaping: Madison Cox & Associates; project manager: Erik Moraillon

- Exhibition hall and bookshop design: Christophe Martin Architectes

- Auditorium design: Findlay Ross, Theatre Projects

- Acoustic design: Victoria Chavez, Theatre Projects

- Restaurant interior design: Yves Taralon

- Lighting design: Akari-Lisa Ishii, I.C.O.N., assisted by Carole Ferreri

- Visual identity and signage design: Philippe Apeloig

- Civil engineering and structural work: Gold Études

- Cost consultants: CB Économie

## Contracting authority assistance

- Programming:
  Arnaud Perrin Programmation
  and Jean-Michel Rousseau

- Preventive conservation consultant:
  Véronique Monnier – X.Art

- Manager: Kevin Kennel

- Clerk of works: Artelia

- Technical inspection agency: Socotec

## Contractors and consultants

General contractor:
Bymaro (subsidiary of Bouygues
Construction in Morocco)

Direction and management:
Ali Bencheqroun, Meryem Hammoumi,
Charaf Soussi, Hind Boutaleb

Project team during the construction phase:
Mohamed Tadili (project manager),
Ali Benazzouz, Saadia Belhousse, Lamyae
Chekkar, Oussama Jarrad, Ghita Benyaich

Project team during the commercial phase:
Karim Chekchouki, Ghizlane El Fath

Architectural lighting:
Arrakis Lighting

## GENERAL INFORMATION

### Location and geographical information

- Location: Rue Yves Saint Laurent,
  Arrondissement de Guéliz, commune
  de Marrakech, Wilaya de Marrakech,
  Kingdom of Morocco

- Orientation: NE

- Prevailing winds:  NW–SE

- Altitude: 450 m (1,475 ft)

### General programme

- Museum with permanent and temporary
  exhibition rooms, bookshop, restaurant,
  auditorium, foyer, gallery, library,
  collection storerooms and offices.
  Public building (300–700 capacity)

### Project timeline

- Research begins: January 2014

- Procurement of building permit:
  August 2014

- Construction begins: September 2015

- Construction complete: May 2017

- Snag list complete: July 2017

- Inauguration: October 2017

- Project duration: 20 months

## Surface areas

- Plot size: 2,630 m² (28,300 ft²)

- Built area: 3,908 m² (42,065 ft²)
  (ground floor: 1,569 m²/16,890 ft²;
  1st floor: 555 m²/5,975 ft²;
  basement: 1,784 m²/19,200 ft²)

- Usable floor area: 3,086 m² (33,215 ft²)
  (ground floor: 1,125 m²/12,100 ft²;
  1st floor: 415 m²/4,465 ft²; basement:
  1,546 m²/16,640 ft²)

## Type of construction

Structure: walls and posts in reinforced
concrete

Foundations: insulated concrete footings

Facades: exterior cladding in natural
terracotta bricks; precast terrazzo base

Sustainability measures: local materials;
double exterior wall with air gap and
insulation; double glazing with solar
protection; rainwater recovery

## Detailed programme

- Large hall: 165 m² (1,775 ft²)

- Permanent exhibition gallery: 340 m²
  (3,670 ft²)

- Temporary exhibition gallery: 120 m²
  (1,290 ft²)

- 128-seat auditorium: 190 m² (2,045 ft²)

- Bookshop: 80 m² (860 ft²)

- Restaurant with terrace: 170 m²
  (1,830 ft² including kitchens)

- Ticket office: 15 m² (160 ft²)

- Offices: 120 m² (1,290 ft²)

- Research library: 40 m² (430 ft²)

- Storerooms for the Yves Saint Laurent
  and Berber Museum collections: 600 m²
  (6,460 ft²)

- Plant rooms: 480 m² (5,165 ft²)

- Circulation, delivery area and
  two-wheeled-vehicle parking
  in the basement: 340 m² (3,660 ft²)

- Staff areas (canteen, changing rooms,
  prayer room, etc.): 215 m² (2,315 ft²)

**Karl Fournier and Olivier Marty wish to thank:**

Madison Cox, who, from initial idea of the book to final layout, constantly supported our project.

The Jardin Majorelle and the Pierre Bergé–Yves Saint Laurent Foundations as well as the Yves Saint Laurent Museum Marrakech.

The Izhak team, for their involvement and the care they took in the creation of this book, particularly Laure Frey and Mickaël Ben David, as well as Nicolas Picard and Thomas Bonometti.

Catherine Sabbah, who accepted the challenge of writing the story of this adventure.

Nathalie Franck for her wise advice.

All members of Studio KO, past and present, who have contributed, sometimes unwittingly, to the development of this work.

Björn Dahlström, Philippe Apeloig, Tom Vidalie, Christophe Martin, Jean-Michel Rousseau, Reda Issolah, Alexis Sornin, Zora Elhajji, Nathalie Guihaumé, Dan Glasser, Jaimal Odedra, Noel Manalili, Yann Deret, André Rau, Jérôme Schlomoff, Hassina Baba-Ali, Miza Mucciarelli, Hervé Micaud, Étienne Baillet, Cyril Lignac and Laurence Mentil, for their valuable contributions.

Our publisher Phaidon – and particularly Emilia Terragni and Hélène Gallois Montbrun, whose enthusiasm for this book has never wavered.

Finally, Fayçal Tiaïba, for his involvement and his passion: without him, this book would never have seen the light of day.

IO

Studio KO          www.studioko.fr          www.aroundko.fr

Phaidon Press Limited
2 Cooperage Yard
London E15 2QR

Phaidon Press Inc.
65 Bleecker Street
New York, NY 10012

phaidon.com

First published 2022
Reprinted 2023
© 2022 Phaidon Press Limited

ISBN 978 1 83866 388 9
ISBN 978 1 83866 414 5 (luxury edition)

A CIP catalogue record for this book is available
from the British Library and the Library of Congress.

Associate Publisher: Emilia Terragni
Project Editor: Hélène Gallois Montbrun
Assistant Editor: Baptiste Roque-Genest
Production Controller: Elaine Ward
Design: Izhak
Translation from French: Anne McDowall for Lunedit.com

The publisher would like to thank Robyn Taylor and
João Mota for their contribution to the book.

Printed in China